Marriage Of
DECEIT

DEDICATION

This book is dedicated to all the women who fear the men in their life. Please do not wait as long as I did to get out of the relationship. It is only now that I fully understand the saying, "God helps those who help themselves."

Thank you to God for giving me the strength to find the way out.

A special thank you to my two guardian angels, Noella and Peter Vachon.

You helped me see the light at the end of the tunnel and I will always be grateful.

R.I.P. Noella

FOREWORD

I WAS SIXTEEN AND CELEBRATING MY ENGAGEMENT. My sister Rose was miserable. Why? Why would your own sister act like this? Out of jealousy, of course. Rose was always jealous of me. She was very selfish. From the time we were kids Rose would be jealous of the dolls I received from my mother, any extra attention my dad or mom would give me, and most of all she was jealous of the relationship I had with my boyfriend, Ken.

A year passed and I was seventeen. It was 1957, and Ken and I were married. I felt like a queen, but little did I know how heavy and painful my role as a wife to him would be.

Seventeen years old and married. I was being bossed around again. First by my parents and now my husband. I was doing everything he wanted me to do. In 1963 our first son was born. Ken made sure he was in control of the children, too. He wandered off into a world of his own after our first son, Mark, was born.

He had friends I had never met, and we were receiving strange phone calls and being sued left and right. What was going on? Was he even working? What was his secret life?

Lacking a husband's love, I wanted a large family. I had so much love to give and he didn't want it. He forbade me to work or go out much, so I proceeded to give all my time and love to my children.

Our house was searched so often by the police. Something was going on and I wasn't allowed to ask questions. He would do strange things like buy bullets and mail them to people. In 1969, Ken came home one day unrecognizable. He was dressed up in a disguise. In 1970 he was arrested for fraud.

I couldn't get much out of my husband. According to Ken, everyone else was wrong, not him.

Five years later, he was arrested again on another fraud charge and for breaking and entering. He hadn't worked for the past fourteen years as we were both on welfare. The man had a vicious temper and I was terrified of him.

Then came the first divorce in 1976. What followed was the biggest mistake of my life—yes, I remarried him in 1981. The fear I had of Ken fooled me into thinking he had changed.

INTRODUCTION

I WAS BORN AT 376-FIRST AVENUE IN VERDUN, Quebec. It was 1940 and I was the fourth child out of six. As a child I was very shy; I used to keep to myself. I had dreams, big dreams. My whole childhood I was known as the dreamer.

My mother worked for part of my childhood. I missed her love and her time. I envied my two older sisters when they started to work because they had nice clothes and boyfriends. I didn't have any of that and I was quite lonely. There was a time in my life from the age of thirteen to fifteen where I wanted to become a nun. What I would have done to become a nun. God was my life. I went around praying for the whole world, praying for everyone's souls, praying they would go to heaven and live the everlasting life. That ended when Ken came into my life.

At fifteen I became very shapely and attractive. My legs were perfect! I would say they were my best asset. I had many boyfriends that year. Unfortunately, I was also very naive.

My hobbies at the time included knitting, reading and dancing, but my big goal that year was to find a boyfriend who would love me and had the potential to be marriage material.

At fifteen-and-a-half I met Ken. He was the man of my dreams. Standing six feet one, with blond hair and blue eyes, this man was simply the sexiest human being I had ever seen in my life. Who would have known that life with him would turn out to be such a nightmare?

FAMILY

I CAN REMEMBER AS CLEAR AS YESTERDAY HOW special my parents were to me when I was a child. Dad was a man who was always working. He was always on the go. When I was around five years old, my mother starting working at the Douglas Hospital in Montreal. She worked at night and my dad was gone working during the day. He was a handyman, and he would fix any shoes that needed repair. Dad would make sure we all had our baths and that all our evening chores were done. Most nights I would ask him to read me a bedtime story and he always obliged. You see, he had these old books of famous fables and I simply loved the way he read them, always reading with excitement in his voice and making everything come alive. To me, my dad was the smartest man alive. He built a country house for us with his bare hands in Cascade Point, thirty miles from where we lived in Verdun. It had two closed bedrooms, a kitchen and a beautiful inside porch. We all loved it there as kids and spent every single summer there from as far back as I can remember.

Mom was a beautiful woman. She was very hard-working and didn't have much time to spend with me because of the fact that she had to work all the time to put food on the table. She used to make us breakfast and then go back to bed. Mom would wake up around noon and start the laundry and all the household work for the day, before she left again to go to work at night. Most of the time I spent with my mother was in the summer, at the cottage.

My sister Helen was the oldest in the family. Joe was the second oldest, Rose the third and then myself. Nine years later, Richard came along, followed by my sister Linda. Linda was the youngest of our family. I got along very well with Helen and Richard. We enjoyed our time together as kids.

I cherish most of my childhood memories. When I was twelve I had a crush on a boy named Brian Green. He was so handsome. Mom didn't know but I went on a few dates with him. It was disappointing because in those days parents used to tag along. Yes! Imagine being at the movies with your boyfriend and their mother sitting right beside you. She was the one paying for the movies, so I guess I couldn't really complain. She liked to come with us because at that time the movie theatre had a promotion where they were giving out certain types of dishes that she liked, and she wanted to collect all of them. My relationship with Brian didn't last long because my parents moved to another town that summer.

I became very studious in school. My marks were excellent—so excellent that on one of my grade-seven term report cards I pulled a 98.6%. I tried out for a scholarship that year. Mom was so proud of me! You should have seen the tears in her eyes! Unfortunately, I didn't win the scholarship, but my marks that year were nonetheless spectacular.

As I approached the age of fourteen, I started to become very religious. I was attending mass every morning and sometimes even every night. I would say the rosary every evening on my knees. I wanted more than anything to become a nun and I was praying for peace for the whole world. All of this lasted until the next year when I turned fifteen. Fifteen would be the year that changed my life forever. I fell in love three or four times when I was fifteen. They were all American boys. Nothing ever became of the relationships, though; they were all summer flings, as they say.

THE BOYFRIEND

ONE NIGHT I WAS AT MY FRIEND CAROL'S PLACE. WE were in her living room watching TV. I glanced over and saw a picture on her TV stand of a handsome young blond man. "Carol," I said. "Who is that dreamboat?" Carol explained to me that it was her twenty-one year old cousin. She said he wasn't interested in meeting anyone because he was engaged to be married. I then said to her that engaged wasn't married and that I just *had* to meet him.

I called him on the telephone and we made a double-date. It was Carol, Eddie, Ken and I who would be going. I couldn't believe he agreed. What did this mean? Was I really going to go through with this? I was so nervous!

The minute I laid eyes on Ken, I fell in love. On our first date the boys came over to Carol's house. We put on music (records at the time) and we danced all night. I didn't want it to end. We had a lot of fun that night. At the end of the night Ken drove me home. He parked across the street from my house. What was I to do? I was so nervous. He pulled me against him. It was so hot and it felt so right. We starting kissing passionately. What a kisser he was! After a couple of minutes, Ken started to put his hand down my pants. I immediately slapped him.

To my astonishment he slapped me right back! I yelled at him and said I wasn't that kind of girl. Ken told me he knew that and could sense it, as well, but if I *ever* laid hands on him again, our relationship would be over. I was totally stunned and didn't say a word.

The second date Ken and I went on, we went driving around. We always ended up eating at a restaurant, which he always paid for. An odd thing occurred on that date. He asked me what I would say to him if he asked me to marry him. I, of course told him, "Ask me and you'll find out." Ken didn't say anything after that; he just smiled.

THE ENGAGEMENT

I FOUND OUT LATER ON THAT WEEK THAT KEN BROKE off his engagement with his fiancée. We dated for about a year and then he proposed. Sixteen years old and I was engaged! It was every young woman's dream at the time. Ken proposed to me on my birthday. It was June 4th, 1956. When I showed my sister Rose the ring, she didn't even look at it. She had gotten engaged a couple of months prior and she in no way wanted the limelight taken away from her. My own sister once again jealous of me. It broke my heart.

Ken took all my time and my love. I was so into him that I never finished high school. I did try taking a typing course but quit because I detested it. I did, however, get a job at Northern Electric working on a printing machine.

Ken had a good job in an office. He told me he had been trained by an accountant since he was thirteen. He didn't have any degrees but I guess he was a fast learner. Life was good. We were young and in love.

Time went by and odd things started happening. A few times a month Ken told me he wouldn't be seeing me that day or that night because he was too busy at work. He explained to me that he had a friend who he knew long before he met me who needed help and a shoulder to cry on. If I only knew then what I know now, I would have left him in a split second, but I didn't. Her name was Gwen Marshall. I became very curious about her. Ken had the audacity to tell me she was very beautiful and had a perfect figure. She was blond and did some modelling from time to time. The modelling was apparently just for fun because her family was very wealthy.

One evening when we were home, Ken told me that Gwen was upset because he told her that he was getting married. I then asked him why she would be upset if they were just friends. He explained to me that Gwen told him that she had hoped one day he would have married her. He said there was never any sex involved and she was only a friend. He also mentioned that he would never marry a wealthy woman. I didn't believe this story—not one bit. I asked to meet Gwen. Ken came home a couple of nights later with his cousin Carol, my friend. He asked Carol to vouch for him if he and Gwen were just friends and she did as he asked. I knew my friend was lying just by the tone of her voice.

THE HAT

THE ODD SCENARIOS DIDN'T STOP THERE. ONE DAY when I saw Carol, she told me she had been to Ken's mother's house for a family dinner. She said that Ken's ex-fiancée's church hat was sitting on a shelf in their house. I found it very odd that he would still have items of hers since their relationship ended a while before we were engaged. When I confronted Ken, he denied it. He said it was his mother's hat. I let it be, until one day I went over to Ken's mother's house and asked her myself. She told me it was not her hat and she had no idea whose it was. Another lie. Why was my fiancé lying to me? What did I do to deserve this?

Ken lived with his parents, one sister and a younger brother. One night when I was on my way over there with Ken, we saw his ex-fiancée Leona leaving the house. Ken asked her where she was going and she replied that she was going home. I was mortified. Why was Leona still coming around? I knew that she still went to church with Ken's mother but this was getting out of control. Ken told me to open the back door of the car for her. I told Ken that if he wanted to drive her home to do so, but I wasn't going to be a part of it. To my surprise Ken then slapped me across the face quite hard and reached over and opened the back door for Leona. Yes, he actually hit me! Leona entered the car in the back and they chatted all the way to her house while never introducing me at all. I was hurt and shocked. How could he do this to me? I was his fiancée. When Leona got out the car, I immediately asked Ken to drive me home. There was no way I was going to spend the rest of the day with a man who just did this to me. He yelled at me all the way home, calling me a sick jealous bitch. I pointed out that it wasn't only the lift but the fact that her hat was still in the house and that he lied about it. I told him I thought he was still seeing her. Of course Ken denied it and I—being a young, naive sixteen-year-old—believed him.

I remember like yesterday the evening we were on our way to our wedding rehearsal. Ken had not arrived yet so my mother decided to have a private talk with me. She said that she had proof that Ken had been flirting with my brother Joe's girlfriend. I was shocked at what my mother said and didn't believe her—after all, he did turn down a beautiful girl like Gwen Marshall to marry me so why would he flirt with my brother's girlfriend?

After the wedding rehearsal I confronted him about it. Ken looked at me and said, "We just came back from our wedding rehearsal and you accuse me of this?" I felt so guilty I didn't say another word.

WEDDING VOWS

We were married September 7th, 1957. It was a fairly large wedding with approximately 150 people in attendance. My dress was so beautiful and Ken didn't look too bad himself. I had so much love in my heart for him that day. I told myself that the other women in Ken's life didn't mean anything because he was now mine forever. I thought so, anyway. After the wedding in the church we all gathered at the reception hall. I was so excited to dance with my husband, to hold him close and cherish our day. But every time I tried to dance with him, he was dancing with another woman—one in particular. She was the daughter of Ken's mother's very good friend. This woman was known as a tart back in our day. I didn't like it because they danced very close. I was so embarrassed and hurt. The day that was supposed to be the happiest day of my life was turning out to be just the opposite. As if things couldn't get any worse, later that night while we were making love, Ken pulled out a condom. I wanted his skin close to mine, I wanted every-thing to be close, I wanted to feel the heat and the passion. I didn't care if I got pregnant; after all, we were married. But he didn't wanted any children, and he made it clear.

For the first year we lived with Ken's parents. We bought a brand-new bedroom set. It was beautiful. I wasn't allowed to work, so I quit my job two months after we were married. Ken didn't want me to work. He wanted me to stay home and cook his meals and do the laundry like a wife should be doing, he said. His mother catered to his every need. It was unbelievable. He was the favourite of all the children and it was evident. I got very bored there and wanted a place of my own, my own privacy with my husband.

After a couple of months passed, I got so fed up that I decided that I wanted to go back to work modelling stock-ings. I had the legs for it and the pay was fantastic. I made an appointment with my friend, Pearl. I was so excited about this opportunity and wanted to share my excitement with my husband, so I told Ken about it. Well, it didn't go over well; he was furious. "No wife of mine will be a model," he said. He told me that my job was to be his wife and he gave me an ultimatum: him or the job. I sobbed and sobbed for days. How could my husband, someone who was sup-posed to be happy for me and supportive, not allow me to do something I wanted to do? I did what I was told and cancelled the interview.

PRIVACY AT LAST

MY HUSBAND WAS A CONSTANT BRAGGER. ON A daily basis he would tell me how lucky I was to have a man like him, someone who didn't smoke or drink. His father was an alcoholic and gave his mother a very hard time. Ken used to break up fights with his parents when he was younger and his dad actually pulled a knife on his mother once because he thought she was sleeping around. Ken said he didn't want to follow in his dad's footsteps and that's why he chose never to drink.

I wasn't happy the first year of our marriage. Instead of being in the honeymoon phase, I was lonely. The only time I was happy were the weekends when we used to go to Plattsburgh, New York. I loved going there, doing some shopping and looking around. It was a change of scenery; I was able to go out and didn't have to cook and do laundry. Ken's favourite place to shop in Plattsburgh was a store where they sold pornographic magazines. He used to buy *Playboy* and *Hustler* magazines all the time. Most of our sex only happened after he looked at those magazines. He had so many of them I stopped counting. He loved going to Plattsburgh because in the 1950s, they didn't sell those magazines in Canada, only in the USA. I expressed my dislike for them and didn't appreciate him wasting money on them. Once again, I was called a jealous bitch.

A place opened up right across the street from Ken's parents. New apartment buildings were being constructed left and right, and Ken wanted to move there so we could have our privacy. I was thrilled! Finally, our own place. Ken signed the lease a couple of weeks later and we went to look for furniture. We already had our bedroom set and a cedar chest we received from our engagement, so we didn't have to worry about those things. Ken wouldn't let me choose the furniture, though. He did, however, give me the choice of which washing machine to get. I was so hurt but didn't express it to him because I was just so happy to be out on our own.

One day when Ken came home from work, he had a surprise for me. He showed up with a very large white rabbit. I was so happy because I loved bunnies, but also a little uneasy because I didn't know how to take care of one. The bunny was very mischievous and chewed all the wires and wood in the apartment. Ken then brought home a smaller black bunny so he could have a friend, but that didn't work out either. The bigger rabbit would hump the smaller one in a show of dominance and they used to fight a lot. I had to eventually give them back to the pet store as I wasn't experienced enough in raising rabbits.

My husband's dream was to become an actor. Ken followed all the stars' lives very closely. Between all the magazines he bought about them and the *Playboys*, I didn't know which he was more obsessed with. Ken told me that he performed in a few plays and was hoping to act again in the future. He explained that to get anywhere in that industry you had to have connections. He said that if you waited for luck or to be discovered that you would get lost in the shuffle and never be successful. Ken explained that actors were a different class of people and that you had to be one to understand what he meant.

THE CHANGE

Time passed and Ken registered a company under the name of Thunderbird Productions. He explained to me that this company would get him where he needed to be in order to build his empire. He went down to the courthouse to do this. Once this was done, Ken opened up a fake bank account under the name of Thunderbird Productions. He then began corresponding with many film companies and actors like Dick Powell. He used fictitious names in writing these letters. All his letters had professional stationary with the company's name on it. He also had stamps of the company's name so he could stamp his own cheques, making it look like he was getting paid by the company.

One of the fictitious names he used was Dan Parker. Dan Parker was the apparent owner of Thunderbird Productions. In the letters he wrote that Dan specified that Ken Robinson was an excellent upcoming actor from Canada and one of his best employees. Ken also enclosed studio pictures in the letters. As Ken was a very good-looking man, I was sure Hollywood would have a place for him.

Some movie studios actually wrote him back. They expressed great interest in meeting my husband. They wrote in the letters that they would be interested in meeting him for an interview whenever he could make it to California. What great news! Ken was thrilled.

First things first: we had to find money to get to California. I was eighteen at the time and Ken was twenty-four. Ken's dream was to become an actor but I wanted children. I discussed having children with him, but Ken had a one-track mind. He wanted to pay off the furniture and then go to California.

I convinced him to let me get a job to speed up the process. I took out an application at Simpsons department store downtown to be a salesperson. I was hired right away. I started off in the lingerie department part-time. It didn't take long before I had a permanent position selling coats in the basement. Ken started to get very jealous for some reason. He would ask me daily if any guys were making passes at me while I was at work. He would drive me to and from work and made sure I called him on my lunch hours. Weekends came and I wanted to have my friends over, but Ken refused to allow this. He told me that I had a new life now and they were not part of it. That's when I started to get lonely, very lonely. The only friends who ever came over were Ken's friend Eddy and his girlfriend. Even Ken's parents didn't come over much and they lived so close by.

My husband was a very unsociable man. We barely went out anywhere. When we did, Ken didn't stay long or pretended he was ill so we could leave. He even went to the extreme one time of punching a door and then telling me his hand was broken and that's why he couldn't go out with me. I was starting to think my husband was losing his mind. This was not normal behaviour. Ken had changed and it was frightening me.

We started seeing Ken's friend Eddy and his girlfriend a couple times a week. They would come over specifically when it was suppertime. Ken would always be so generous to them, buying takeout food, hamburgers and fries with BBQ chicken. The food was great, don't get me wrong, but there was no need for them to mooch from us three to four times a week.

I expressed my frustration that Ken was wasting a lot of money on takeout when we had bills to pay. We were paying for furniture, we had car payments and we were saving for California at the same time. Ken didn't have any friends, really. He was a loner. All he did was read. Among his favourite reading material were books about hunting, pornographic magazines and autobiographies of actors. The man I married was turning out to be a controlling, jealous and paranoid man.

I enjoyed my job at Simpsons. I would meet a lot of new people on a daily basis. It got me away from my husband and I felt alive. I loved being at work because home was boring. All I did was do laundry and cook for Ken. He never helped me with either. He said it was my job as a wife to do these things. The only jobs he thought were his were painting and spring cleaning. Very seldom would he wash a dish. Suppertime would come and I would cook and do up all the dishes while he sat there reading the newspaper. After supper, he would ask me to comb his hair and scratch his back. This type of behaviour made me very sad. Not once did he think about me, how I was also at work on my feet all day at Simpsons. I was starting to feel more like his maid than his wife.

As time went on, I wanted children more and more. Four years passed and every time I talked to Ken about having a baby, he shut down the idea. His excuse was that children were too expensive and that they would tie us down.

I started to knit baby clothes and daydream about having children. If Ken liked it or not I was going to find a way to have kids. Knitting was very soothing for me. I loved it and was very talented.

One evening Ken invited his boss and his wife over for dinner. I felt so uncomfortable that evening. Ken kept bragging all night about the furniture we had and all his future plans. His plans were not my plans. Ken's only goal was getting to California and mine was to start raising a family.

I loved my husband but my marriage was empty. All he did was watch television and talk about movie stars. We never talked about our future together. It was always about him and what he wanted and needed. Once in a blue moon he would take me to the movies, but even that was annoying because at the end of the movie he would insist on giving his opinion about the director and actors as if he was a professional.

When the holidays came around, we always went to my mother's house. All of my family was there. It was nice with all the grandchildren. My heart was heavy, though, seeing them and not being able to have my own kids. I told my sister Helen how much I wanted to be a mother and she smiled and reassured me that I was still young and had plenty of time to do so. Little did she know how Ken felt about the subject. Why was I married to this man? Why was my self-esteem so low that I needed to stay in an unhealthy relationship?

CALIFORNIA

It was 1962; five years had passed in our marriage. Ken had finally decided to make the move to California. At the same time, my sister Rose had given birth to a beautiful baby girl named Sandra. I was a proud godmother and on my way to Cali. We got our passports together, sold our furniture and stored our linen and dishes at Ken's parents' house. I was lucky enough to win a trip to New York City from my work by getting the most accounts opened by new customers. My boss exchanged the trip for money as he knew I was moving and could use the cash. I then took a leave of absence, in case I needed to return back to work one day if things didn't work out.

Off we went in Ken's sports car. We drove to Toronto first to say goodbye to my sister Helen. After driving for five hours, Ken decided to stay the weekend and advised that driving all the way to Cali would be too uncomfortable and he wanted to fly instead. We paid my sister for the stay, as she needed the money with the kids, and continued on our journey. We didn't have an abundance of cash but we sure had a lot of credit cards. Ken had them under his name as well as under the name of his so-called company, Thunderbird Productions.

Our flight to Cali was not a direct flight. It was my first flight ever, so I was very nervous but excited at the same time. We flew on a Viscount plane. One engine stopped while we were flying, so the pilot made the decision to go back to the airport. Great! My first flight and this happens? I was so scared but never showed my fear to Ken. Soon enough, we boarded another plane. It took us a while between all the stops, but eventually we made it to Ken's dream place of California. I really hoped Ken would succeed as an actor down here. I was trying to stay positive.

We rented a car upon arrival. Ken then drove to a large motel on Sunset Boulevard in Hollywood. It was quite a long drive and I was very hot. All I could see was desert in front of me and I never thought we would get there. It seemed like forever, but after driving for about forty-five minutes, I started to see the beauty of the state. I started to get butterflies. Soon enough, we were driving past beautiful palm trees—boy, this place was indeed heaven!

Once we got to the motel, the first thing Ken did was telephone his parents. He never let me use the phone and

I didn't dare ask because he was the one who controlled all the money. It was only in late afternoon that he asked me if I wanted to call mine. I was hurt because he should have asked me right away, even before he called *his* mother in the morning. Unbelievable.

We toured as tourists do, doing a lot of sightseeing. Every night Ken always came back to the motel and ate dinner at the same restaurant downstairs. I thought he was boring to do so but never said anything to him about it.

One night at dinner, I noticed that we were actually sitting next to Ron Ely, the actor who played Tarzan in the TV series. I couldn't believe my eyes! Ken asked me if I would like to meet him and, of course, I said yes.

Ken went over to Ron's table. He was having dinner with another male friend at the time. He introduced himself and they talked for a bit. I was so curious to know what they were talking about. What could my husband actually have to say to this man? Ken finally waved me over to come to the table. I was so shy. Once at the table, Ken introduced me to Ron and then Ron invited us both to sit and join him. Ron shook my hand and I remember thinking he was one of the most handsome men I had ever seen in my life. He actually lit my cigarette for me! I was the happiest woman on earth at that moment. I mean, it's not every day you get to meet Ron Ely.

What a thrill! We all chatted for about a half an hour and then Ron had to depart. It was a night I would never forget.

Back in the motel room, I asked Ken how he got Ron to speak with us. He told me that he introduced himself to Ron as a Canadian movie director looking for American talent to do a movie in Canada. He *what?* I wasn't impressed with Ken's deceit in the least but didn't say anything.

Ken's mood and attitude changed as the days passed when we were in Cali. He told me that it would be useless to go to any movie studios because he had gained so much weight and no one would hire him anymore and the only role he would be cast for would be Dumbo the elephant.

I found it very annoying that Ken would call his parents on a daily basis. It seemed as if he couldn't do anything without calling them. A lost little boy was what he acted like; he was very insecure. I didn't let it bother me too much, though. Our motel had an extremely large pool. Most days I would just sit around and tan. The sun was lovely, the weather was hot all the time . . . who could ask for anything more!

I wish my husband would have relaxed and come swimming with me but he never did. He never once put on a bathing suit. He stayed by the pool always fully dressed, saying his legs were too white. I told him they would always stay white if they never saw the sun, but he said I was stupid for saying such a thing.

While we were in California, Ken received a phone call from his parents. They said that a bank inspector had come to the house asking for Ken. Ken gave some excuse to his parents so they could deal with the situation. To Ken's surprise, his parents said that they paid the bank inspector. Well, was he furious! He said that they shouldn't have done this because he could have gotten away with not paying, but now he had to pay them back.

After that phone call, Ken told me we were leaving California. I said to myself, "Is this man insane?" I reminded him that we had our working papers and could easily find jobs in California. When we made the money back we could wire his parents what he owed and that would be the end of it. Ken said he didn't want his parents taking the responsibility of his debts and nothing I said would change his mind.

Before I knew it, Ken had booked our flight back home and was telling everyone that I was the one who wasn't happy in California. I asked him why he was lying and he said to me that he couldn't tell anyone about the bank issue. I hated coming home. I wanted Ken to break away from his parents. I wanted him to be self-sufficient and to take care of me and give me children—he knew my dream was to become a mother. But from the looks of it, it didn't seem as if that was going to happen.

BIZARRE BEHAVIOUR

KEN KNEW HOW DISAPPOINTED I WAS. I DIDN'T SPEAK with him at all on the plane ride home. Why should I? After all, this was his idea, his dream. Ken seemed too happy coming home. None of this made any sense to me. How in the world could he be happy to return home when it was his big dream to go to California? The visas and the working papers we got were all for nothing.

When we arrived at his parents' house, they gave us a room to ourselves like we'd had before we left. Ken found a job in about a week and I returned to Simpsons. My boss, however, said he was transferring me to the third floor where selling coats was only based on commission. Where I worked in the basement, I had a base salary plus commission, so this was a little frightening for me.

I accepted his offer and actually did very well. My pay-cheques started rolling in and a few of them were actually more than Ken's. Days passed and we had the same old routine. Ken's car started to go on the fritz and when that happened, he always called a cab. "Buses are for peasants," he used to say. I knew the real reason he wouldn't take the bus, though. Ken also talked about how buses were full of germs. He was a paranoid freak. He also didn't want anyone knowing he had a car that wasn't working.

If the taxi was late, Ken would make such a scene. He would walk back and forth, up and down the hallway, then run to the front door to see if it was there. If it wasn't there within two to three minutes, he would keep calling the depot until the taxi showed up. While waiting, he would pound on the wall yelling, "Why me? Why me?" I couldn't' believe his behaviour. He acted like an animal.

Another time, Ken was looking out the window when he noticed the hubcaps on his car were missing on one side. He figured that the person who took them would return for the ones on the other side the next night, so Ken said he would wait for them. I was quite distraught at the fact that he sat up three nights in a row by the door on a chair with a loaded shotgun! Yes, you read correctly: a loaded shotgun. Ken had a licence to carry guns. Another one of his dreams was to be a private investigator. He owned a twelve-gauge shotgun, a .44 Magnum and a .38 revolver. He also owned several bullets. On the third night while he was sitting by the door, he finally saw the two guys coming back for the hubcaps.

Once they were close to his car, Ken opened the front door with his shotgun by his side and didn't say a word. They saw him and took off so fast! It was actually kind of amusing, but at the same time I was terrified at my husband's behaviour.

The word got around on the street that my husband had a shotgun and he wasn't afraid to use it. The neighbours upstairs were afraid to put the garbage out. They would sneak outside and always look around to see if Ken was watching. My husband seemed to enjoy this.

Time passed and life went on. Ken and I continued to work to pay off our credit cards and the money Ken owed from personal loans he had. It took about a year, but we cleared our debt and started looking for a place of our own.

We found a nice upper duplex on 43rd Avenue. It was very spacious and clean, and the rent was affordable. It didn't take long before we signed a lease and moved in. Ken picked out all our furniture again, but he did allow me to pick out the washing machine. What joy! I did speak up sometimes and asked him why he was so controlling, even about furniture. My response from my husband was that I was a spoiled bitch and very ungrateful. I should have been grateful that he took the time to pick out the furniture, was what I was told.

THE ULTIMATUM

K EN AND I HAD BEEN MARRIED FOR SIX YEARS NOW;
I was twenty-two and how I wanted a baby! My relationship
with my husband was slowly getting worse. I wanted a baby
to force my husband to mature and hopefully bring us closer
again. I confronted him about us having children again and
reminded him about the promise he made to me years ago.
He finally agreed to try.

I had my yearly checkup with the gynecologist and let him
know of my plan to conceive. Dr. Bailey wished me luck and
off I was planning my little family. As soon as I got home,
I rushed to my calendar and checked off the three best days
to conceive for that month. The first day I asked Ken if he
wanted to make love and he asked me why. Ken was usually
the one to initiate sex, not me, so I guess he found it odd
that I was asking him. I told him I wanted to try for a baby.
What happened next was so embarrassing— Ken refused
me and said he was too tired.

The second night, he said he had a headache and the third night he was sick to his stomach. I was heartbroken. I locked myself in the bathroom and balled like a baby. After about twenty minutes, I went back to bed and cried some more. My husband heard me. I knew he did and he didn't even say one bloody word.

A couple of months passed and Ken always wanted to use condoms when we had sex. I found myself arguing all the time about having a baby. I had my calendar marked so we could try to conceive on the perfect days each month, but as you can guess, my husband always had an excuse not to do so.

Five years passed. I was becoming very desperate for a child. I was empty and so alone. I even threatened to leave Ken if he would keep preventing us from conceiving when we made love. He had his hunting, his fishing and his TV shows, and I had nothing. I wasn't allowed to go anywhere, not with my friends and not to visit family, either. The only place Ken allowed me to go was to his sister's house to knit. I had to find a way to tell my husband I needed a baby. What could I lose by saying something? I had nothing now, anyway. I found the courage one night to tell him that if he didn't give me at least one baby to love then I was going to leave him for good. I reminded him of the promise he made to me and then I started to pack my clothes in a suitcase.

I was petrified of his response, but I didn't care anymore. I had to take a chance. I was desperate for a child.

"Ann," he said, "Come over here." As I walked over to him, he grabbed me passionately, and we started kissing. He slowly started caressing me and we made love three times that night. Now this was what I wanted!

I missed my period that month. I called Dr. Bailey and told him but he said only to let him know if I missed two months in a row. The second month went by with no sign of menstruation. Back I went to the doctor, and he confirmed that I was pregnant! Dr. Bailey actually said to me that I would be getting a nice Christmas present. I didn't catch on at first and asked him what exactly he meant. He confirmed the baby would be due around Christmas—the 21st of December, to be exact. I started to cry tears of joy. I left the office, rubbed my tummy and told my unborn child how much I loved him or her. I started wearing dresses that made my tummy look even bigger than it was. I was so proud to be expecting. My face was glowing and I was finally happy!

My husband was very cold during my pregnancy. He didn't seem happy at all. The larger my belly became, the more disgusting he said I looked. He said people used to tell him that pregnant women were beautiful but he didn't agree at all. To him I was fat and appalling. I cried and cried. He said it wasn't my fault and that it was just his opinion.

I couldn't believe that a human being could be so cruel to his own wife.

I continued to work for a couple of months until Ken ordered me to quit. He wanted me to be at home and cater to his every need. A woman's place was in the home, he said, nowhere else. I applied for unemployment right away. They gave it to me, but I had to hide my belly every time I went in for an appointment because back then you weren't allowed to be on unemployment when you were expecting a child. To the government this meant you would not be available for work. Either your husband had to support you or you had to work until the end of your pregnancy.

Ken told me that his friend Gwen thought he was stupid for getting me pregnant, yet in the same breath, he told me she was buying us a playpen for the baby. "Good," I said. "When will I meet her?" He told me not yet because she was still hurt that he didn't marry her and chose me instead. He also mentioned to me that he and Gwen believed that all people on earth were controlled by a super force, somewhere in outer space. Unknown creatures were playing with us like little toys. He said they were very mean, and that when they were finished with us they would destroy us. Apparently, that's where death came in. I didn't take Ken's talk too seriously as I just thought he was putting me on. He never introduced me to Gwen ever, after all this strange talk.

The thought entered my mind that this woman had to be his girlfriend on the side. What was he hiding and why? What did I do to deserve this treatment? Whenever I confronted him, he would tell me I was a jealous, filthy-minded bitch. I was so fed up from being spoken to that way that I stopped asking to meet her altogether.

THE BIRTH

THE TIME WAS COMING SOON FOR ME TO HAVE THE baby. I was about seven-and-a-half months pregnant and my family had a baby shower for me. The gifts I received were so beautiful. It was everything I ever wanted. I was spoiled and so happy that I was finally going to have the child I had always dreamed of.

I was started to regret marrying Ken. Besides his being so physically distant during the pregnancy, he was also very distant in his thoughts, and everything else he did. Most nights he would sneak out and come back very late at night, always stating that he'd had to work late. I didn't believe him but never wanted to bring it up because I knew it would cause an argument. Towards the end of my pregnancy, my husband was growing more and more impatient. He wanted me to speak to the doctor and have him break my water because his anxiety was getting too high. I never called the doctor but led him to believe I did and that the doctor said he was too busy to take me in. Anything to shut him up.

My last visit to Dr. Bailey was on the 19th of December, 1963. He told me I could possibly go the 29th before giving birth. With that in mind, I still had a couple of Christmas items to shop for, so Ken and I decided we were going shopping. It was Dec 21st and I was in the bathroom getting ready. As I was brushing my hair, I felt something wet in my underwear. I checked and noticed there was some blood. I let Ken know this and he immediately called a cab to bring me to the hospital.

I was in labour for a total of nine hours. Ken didn't help much by pacing back and forth and continuously asking when was I going to push this baby out because he had to get back to work. He didn't seem to have any sympathy for me during this time, nor in the last stages when I was in agony; he actually yelled at me that I was making too much noise and was scaring the lady next to us, who was also in labour in the same room.

After a long nine hours, my son Mark was finally born. There he was, my beautiful baby boy—seven pounds, eight ounces of pure joy! Christmas of '63 was spent in the hospital, but it sure was the best Christmas I ever had! The day we left the hospital with Mark, he slept all the way home. He was a very good baby and never fussed much unless he was hungry. Ken was happy for this, as well. Everything seemed to be going well even though Ken didn't spend much time at home with us.

One morning, I awoke to the phone ringing and ringing. I knew it couldn't be good news, as it was quite early and people rarely called our home. It was my sister Rose calling me to tell me that my niece Debbie had been in a terrible accident. She was hit by a car. Debbie was only five years old at the time. I asked her where Debbie was and she advised me she was lying unconscious at the Montreal Children's Hospital. She had gone to the corner store in Verdun for milk, and while crossing one of the streets, a car had come flying around the corner and hit her. She was thrown in the air only to come crashing down straight on her cranium. The ambulance came immediately and rushed her to the hospital, where they took her straight to the operating table. There, they had to scrape out the part of brain that was damaged and hemorrhaging. She lay unconscious after the operation for a month. No visitors were allowed except her parents, we were told. I was devastated that I couldn't see my niece. I wanted to be there for moral support. I decided to go to church every morning and pray for her. God would hear my prayer. He would have to help her; she was only five years old.

Between the stress of my niece and my son Mark's colic, I was totally exhausted. As I was changing Mark's diaper one day, I started to notice that my vision was impaired. I called Ken at work to tell him and he told me to call our eye doctor. I did and Dr. Conroy asked me to come in that very same afternoon. He performed some tests and referred me to an eye surgeon the following day. I went back the very next day to the surgeon and he did more tests. I was there for quite a while that day. The end result was I was admitted to the hospital immediately because I was going blind in one eye.

STRESS AND DECEIT

KEN BROUGHT MY CLOTHES AND I WAS ADMITTED into my room. I was in a double with an elderly lady who was tied up in a crib. The way she was moaning scared the hell out of me. I asked the nurse why she was tied up and also the reason for her being in a crib. I was told she just had an operation on her eyes and they didn't want her falling out of bed and hurting herself. She was moaning because she was in pain. I understood all of this but it was still very disturbing.

I cried every day for not being able to see my niece and also for not being able to take care of my baby Mark. I missed him so much. The days passed, and with each day, I was losing more and more of my sight in my left eye. I was petrified. The doctor had ordered so many tests and having to take them exhausted me.

After a couple of days of tests we found out that nothing was horribly wrong and that it was my nerves that had brought on the temporary blindness. The hospital administered some medication and my sight slowly started to return. I was finally allowed to return home. We also found out that my niece Debbie would live, but that she would have a lot of rehabilitation to go through and would never fully recover. A quarter of her brain was taken out because of all the hemorrhaging. Once she was out of the hospital, she would have to learn all over again how to walk, talk and eat by herself.

Home sweet home. Upon my return, I was amazed to find my son Mark dressed all in matching colours. I found this very suspicious because Ken never took the time to match anything, never mind baby clothes. Once again, I didn't question my husband because he would only start arguing with me.

Each day that passed, Ken grew more and more distant with me. We seldom made love anymore and even when we did, Ken was distant then, as well. I asked my husband many times what was bothering him. I even told him if he had met another woman and cared for her we could discuss it. What was his response to that? Same old usual screaming and calling me a filthy-minded bitch who thought about nothing but sex. Talking to him was useless.

Eventually, Ken started going out twice a week in the evenings. The reason for this, he said, was that his friend Frank had hired him as his accountant. He would do his books when asked. Each time before he left, I would ask for Frank's telephone number. Ken never gave it to me, saying that I would only be bothering him. He did call me when he was out, but it sounded like a tape recording. He would always say, "Hi, anyone call? Is Mark okay? Fine, see you later. Bye."

Two nights turned into five and sometimes seven nights a week. It was really getting out of hand. His excuses turned into that he needed to drive around and think, or he was taking acting lessons.

I sat alone night after night, thinking how empty our marriage had become I mean, it was never terrific, but now? What was left? I craved for another child. I had so much love to give and my husband didn't want it. I needed to fill the emptiness, and for me another child was the solution.

By this time Ken has made a den for himself in our spare room. I was forbidden to smoke in there. My husband didn't smoke and he detested people who did, especially when they did it around him. He purchased a new double bed and placed it in the den. That bed was more comfortable than the one we had in our own bedroom! He said it would be for guests. I found it odd, as we never had anyone over. Once again, my suspicions were correct as he was the one sleeping in it night after night.

It took me about a year to talk Ken into giving me another child. I wanted a sibling for Mark to play with and was hoping Ken would turn into more of a family man. That didn't seem to be the case, as once again I was beaming with joy when I found out I was pregnant and Ken seemed more distant than ever. Our lovemaking decreased to every other month—no passion, no feeling involved—it just seemed as if he felt it was his duty to satisfy me every other month or so. I didn't and couldn't understand why my own husband didn't want me, didn't want our family.

With his job as an accountant, my husband claimed he would soon be needing a secretary. He said I didn't have the brains to help him, so that was out of the question. He was hoping to eventually find a good one at one of his jobs and hire her for himself. I was pre-warned that regular lunches with his secretary would be normal and not to get jealous. Who would say something like that? What was he trying to tell me? He said he would have to test a lot of women out, so if he was seen in public with different women I should know that they were all just potential job candidates and not to be alarmed. Really? I couldn't believe what had just come out of my husband's mouth. I was so disappointed I just went to bed that night and cried myself to sleep.

One evening, Ken came home from work and told me to pack my bags because we were leaving for Florida. I knew we couldn't afford it and asked him how we were going to pay for it. He told me his friend Gwen was paying for everything. Apparently Gwen owned a hotel in Miami Beach. She had been trying to get Ken to purchase land out there for years. He said he couldn't tell Gwen that he was broke. After all, he had his pride.

ON THE ROAD AGAIN

OFF TO FLORIDA WE WENT: KEN, MARK, AND ME. At this time, I was about three months pregnant with my second child. It wasn't easy travelling with a three-year-old. We couldn't really enjoy our vacation because Mark always gave us a hard time in the restaurants, so we ended up mostly eating in the hotel room. The weather was hot and beautiful during our stay, so that was a plus, at least. One evening, at bath time, I heard a knock at the door. I didn't like answering the door when Ken wasn't there, so I asked who it was while I looked out the peephole. It was the maid, so I opened the door. "Miss Gwen asked me to bring you this," she said. I thanked her politely and closed the door. Why was Ken's friend Gwen sending over a padded rubber shirt for our son? Why didn't she bring it herself? The biggest question of all was why hadn't I met her yet? When Ken came back to the room later that night, I questioned him about it. I also asked him to finally introduce me to her. "We'll both be invited to an elegant dinner one night, so you can meet her before we leave," he said. Frankly, I didn't think this was ever going to happen, but I really wanted to believe my husband.

The phone rang. I immediately got up to get it and Ken screamed at me not to touch it. He said he was waiting for a very important long-distance phone call. He answered it. I couldn't really hear what he was saying because he was talking so softy and sweetly—the way a man would speak to his girlfriend or wife. During the phone call, Mark was playing and making noise, and Ken signalled me to keep him quiet. I did as I was told.

When he finished his conversation, I asked him who he had been speaking to. He told me it was Gwen from Paris.

"Isn't she at the hotel?" I asked.

"She was, but she left," Ken said. You'll have to meet her another time."

I then questioned my husband as to why he spoke to her so softly and always screamed at me. He said she didn't make him angry like I did. Well, that didn't go over well. We had quite the argument after that, and once Ken felt cornered with my questions he got up, once again called me a filthy-minded, ugly bitch, and slapped me right across the face! I cried and cried. After about twenty minutes of crying, my husband apologized.

We stayed in Florida for about a week. I did a lot of sunbathing at the pool and Mark had fun, as well. Ken was always gone during the day "on business," he said. The week went by fast and it was time to return home. The flight back was quite pleasant, as Mark didn't give us much trouble this time.

GWEN

I STARTED KNITTING A LOT AT NIGHT AS KEN WAS never home and I didn't have much to do. My days were kept busy caring for Mark, but the nights were getting pretty lonesome. I had a knitting buddy, Ken's sister, Diane. She would come over quite frequently as she lived right next door to us. It was pretty convenient and we enjoyed each other's company.

One night I was awakened by the telephone. It was after 1 a.m. Ken bolted out of bed so fast it frightened me. I asked him who it was and he covered the mouthpiece and told me to mind my own fucking business. Me, his wife, told to mind my own business. I turned around and cried myself to sleep once again.

Ken stayed on the phone for over an hour. I walked by him multiple times to go and get water and when I did, I overheard him saying to whoever he was on the phone with, that I was fat and distorted because of my pregnancy.

I was so angry that I wanted to pack my bags, take my son and leave him for good. I went back to bed, and about fifteen minutes later, Ken got off the phone. He told me he'd been on the phone with his secretary. Ken said she had just broken up with her husband and needed his advice. I was so tired that I didn't even question it. I went back to sleep.

It was my last month of pregnancy. I was growing more and more excited. Was I having another boy or would it be a girl this time? I chose the name Susan for a girl and David for a boy. One afternoon, I received a long-distance call. It was from a man who claimed he was in Florida and needed to relay an urgent message to Ken. Ken was still at the office at the time so I asked him what the message was and said that I would give it to Ken when he came home. I was told that Gwen had been in a terrible car accident. The man hung up the phone so fast that I wasn't able to inquire any further. I immediately called my husband at work to tell him the horrible news. I wasn't even able to say two words, however, because the minute he heard my voice he started screaming at me, saying I had no right calling him at work when he was busy. He said he wasn't lazy like me, sitting at home all day, doing nothing. I still gave him the message, anyway, figuring he was just having a bad day.

When he came home that evening, Ken told me he would have to leave for Florida. I told him I wanted to come so

I could finally meet Gwen. I just had to see if this woman even existed or if it was all made-up lies. I had been hearing about Gwen for years, yet I had never met or spoken with this woman. The only piece of evidence that she existed was a picture in my husband's wallet of her. It looked like a picture taken out of a magazine. I loved my husband and wanted to trust him, but he made it hard with all his excuses and fabricated stories.

Ken made his phone calls, arranging the flight and hotel. He told me that Gwen was lying unconscious in the hospital because she was thrown off a horse. He had to get down there as soon as possible because he couldn't live with himself if she died, and he wasn't there. He told me to call him if and when the baby was born. He said his parents would be there to help me if I decided I needed any help. I didn't even bother to ask him if I could come because, by that conversation, it was clear I wasn't wanted. As usual, before he left he made a big scene, yelling at me and saying I was jealous of his friend who was dying in the hospital. He called his parents that night to say goodbye and at the same time refused a lift to the airport. Ken took a taxi and I sat there, wondering why there were two stories about how Gwen got her injury. First, she was in a car accident, but now she was thrown from a horse? I spent another lonely night, crying myself to sleep.

Ken was gone and I was left with Mark and a second baby on the way any day now. I followed my daily routine of taking care of Mark. What I did do differently, however, was check the mail. When Ken was home, I was forbidden to go check the mailbox or open any mail. I took advantage of this when he was gone, let me tell you! I started going through some of my husband's opened mail. I was shocked when I discovered all the bills we had, including the hotel bill from Florida which Gwen was supposed to have covered. I found all sorts of bills—bills for jewellery (which I never received), bills for flowers (also not for me) and bills for different restaurants, as well. I hated spying on my husband, but I had to know the truth.

His trip lasted two weeks. When Ken came home, he was very quiet, which wasn't normal for him. He told me Gwen never regained consciousness after her fall off the horse and she died a couple days after. Ken said one day he would find that horse and kill it. I couldn't believe what I was hearing. His story seemed so far-fetched, but once again I gave my husband the benefit of the doubt even though I still had that phone call in the back of my mind that she'd had a car accident.

Ken went on to tell me that Gwen left him all of her estate. He said it would take about six months to sell everything before he could see any money from it. He also showed me a letter from a trust company showing that he had about a quarter of a million dollars coming to him. I thought to myself that Gwen must have been real after all. But why was she always hidden? And why was he so ashamed of me?

These questions kept running through my brain day after day. I couldn't bring them up with Ken because he would only yell and scream at me like he always did. I kept all my emotions inside and stayed silent. Our second child was another boy. I was happy. I wanted to name him David, but Ken insisted that we name him Shawn. Mark now had a little brother he would be able to play with.

THE ABUSE

TAKING CARE OF TWO CHILDREN ALONE EXHAUSTED me. I started to lose a lot of weight. Day and night, I was alone with the children. Ken worked all day and most nights he wasn't home either, always making an excuse that he had meetings or needed his time alone. If I would dare complain that I was tired, he would throw it in my face that I was the one who wanted children and I had to do my job. Only once in a while would he feed Shawn the bottle. While doing so, he would talk to him, telling him how Daddy knows best how to feed and burp him, better than Mommy. I thought he was childish and just ignored him.

One morning I awoke to the doorbell. I looked out the window and didn't recognize the person standing outside. I asked who he was and he informed me he was a bailiff of the court and needed to tow the car away. I immediately called Ken at work to tell him and he replied very calmly to let him do his job. I was so embarrassed but did as he said.

That night Ken came home at suppertime and was very cranky. He was more irritated than he usually was. My husband was rarely in a good mood anyway. He mumbled that he didn't care about the car because he was planning on buying a new one.

Ken had started taking the bus to work. He was so paranoid of germs that every night when he walked through the door, the first thing he would do was take antibiotics. At this time Ken knew a pharmacist who used to sell him antibiotics under the table—mostly penicillin. He had a stock in the house for years. It was unbelievable. He also had a habit of washing his hands many times a day. We needed to have a stash of paper towels in the house at all times. The same went for Coca-Cola soft drinks and May West cakes. If we ran short of any of this, he would start punching the wall and calling me a lazy bitch because I didn't buy them for him. If I would argue with him, he would try and choke me. That's when my fear of my husband became a serious reality.

Ken's secretary gave birth to a baby girl. Ken wanted to look like a hero so he asked me to pack up all the girl baby clothes I received from my baby shower because he wanted to give her a gift. I told him I didn't want to in case we had a baby girl in the future. He screamed at me that we had enough kids and he didn't want more. Hearing this from my husband, I packed the clothes in a bag for him. Off he went to go and visit his secretary with our baby clothes as his gift.

My husband came home later that evening, ranting and raving how I was a stupid bitch and wasn't going to inherit any of Gwen's money if I didn't smarten up. He said that he had ordered flowers for his secretary as another part of her gift and that I had better not complain about it. He was going on and on about her husband—how he was an illiterate bum and wasn't good enough for her. I told him that her marriage wasn't any of his business. Well, that was a mistake! He ran up to me and put his hands around my throat and started choking me. I begged him to stop and ran into the bedroom and started to cry. This man was seriously crazy. I couldn't believe my husband would do something like this to his own wife. He obviously had feelings for his secretary—that was obvious—but treating me so horribly and physically abusing me? What was I to do?

Not too long after this incident, a neighbour of mine came over for coffee. Her name was Sheila. Sheila and I talked for hours. One question she asked, in particular, stuck in my mind. She asked me where my husband worked. When I told her, she said to me that she knew it was him. I didn't understand what she was saying to me at first. Sheila then told me that her good friend just quit her job after having her baby because her boss was obsessed with her. She didn't feel comfortable working for him anymore on account of his behaviour. I was flabbergasted at this accusation towards my husband.

A few days later I approached Ken, letting him know what was said about him and asking him if he had feelings for his ex-secretary. He immediately started screaming at me, calling me a filthy-minded bitch who was probably sleeping with the mailman. He then began to choke me and asked *me* if I was cheating on him! I could hardly breathe but managed to utter a disbelieving *no*.

One morning while I was changing Shawn's diaper, I spotted a bug in his bed. I found it strange as I never seen his type of bug before. I let Ken know about the bug and he told me I was seeing things. Sure enough, the following night, Ken woke up in the middle of the night complaining that something bit him, but when we turned on the light we didn't find anything. I waited until morning when Ken had left for work and rechecked the bed again, finding two bugs that looked exactly the same as the one in Shawn's bed. I put them in a jar and brought them to an exterminator. Just as I had suspected, I was told we had bedbugs. I was mortified.

Ken had the inspector come to see the landlord downstairs the next day. He examined the whole house and came back upstairs to tell us that there was indeed an infestation of bedbugs. Our house only had a few, but it was the eggs he was worried about. He told us to wash everything in hot water and he also fumigated both apartments. Apparently, the landlord's daughter had rented fur coats for her winter wedding. All the coats were placed on the beds and this is apparently how we got them. They infested the landlord's house and eventually made their way upstairs through the walls to us.

Every night for the next two weeks I was scratching myself in paranoia that I had bugs on me. It took a toll on me mentally. Thinking of the bugs made me sick, and I was very glad when I didn't see any more of them.

That month I was late for my period. Ken was furious. He didn't want another child. He made it very clear that we couldn't afford any more children and that if I was pregnant, I had to get an abortion. I reminded him about the inheritance from Gwen that we were expecting and that everything would work out. He then grabbed me by the throat and threw me on the bed, commanding that if I was pregnant I needed to abort it. I couldn't scream or cry because I was choking. He left me there alone with two children standing next to me, crying.

Once I was able to breathe again, I went to bed. My stomach was in a lot of pain that night and for the next couple of days, as well. I decided to go to the doctor to get checked to see if I actually was pregnant. I was worried, too, because I started to bleed a little on a daily basis. Sure enough, Dr. Bailey confirmed I was indeed pregnant and admitted me to the hospital right away for complete bed rest.

THE MISCARRIAGE

KEN DIDN'T LIKE THIS AT ALL. HIS MOTHER WATCHED the boys while he was at work during the day. My husband never came to visit me. He used to call me every day, checking to see if I had lost the baby or not. The more I talked to him on the phone about wanting to keep the baby, the angrier he became. He said to me that he should cut it out himself with a rusty knife. He said he was tired of watching the boys and I needed to hurry up and lose the baby so I could come back home and take care of the children. Every time that he called, I cried. I was losing more and more blood every day. After being in the hospital nearly two weeks, Dr. Bailey finally came into my room to tell me I was losing the baby. He said I had to get up and move around to speed up the process.

I was so depressed. Here I was losing a baby and no one gave a shit. My own husband couldn't wait until I lost it and the doctor also seemed to feel the same way. Dr. Bailey said

I would have to lose it naturally. He signed a release paper and sent me home. I was placed in a taxi and off I went.

I was very happy to return to my boys. They were also very happy to see me. I thanked Ken's mom for watching them. She said they were angels but she was tired because Ken also had her watching them at night when he went out. He usually didn't get back home until very late, she said. That could only mean one thing: my husband had been out gallivanting with another woman while I was losing his third child! It was obvious Ken didn't want my love or time anymore, so I started to feel indifferent.

The night I came home from the hospital, Ken wasn't home, and he didn't show up at all that evening. I decided to watch TV because it was nice and quiet when the kids went to bed. While I was watching TV, I started getting terrible cramps. I ran to the bathroom and noticed I was starting to hemorrhage. I couldn't reach Ken because, again, he never gave me a number for emergencies. I felt a weird sensation and realized I had just lost the baby in the toilet. I was frightened and felt so weak. I was so scared that I flushed the toilet. I peeked before it went down the drain and saw that it was a greyish shape and about the size of my fist. I put a towel under myself and called the doctor right away. He told me I should have kept it as they do studies on miscarriages, but it was too late for that. I got dressed and called Ken's mother to tell her what happened. She told me she would call Ken right away. A few minutes later, she told me that she was on her way over, but Ken was also coming home to watch the boys while I went to the hospital. Imagine that: Ken's mother being able to contact him and not his own wife. Tears fell from my face as I got in a taxi to go to the hospital. Here I was, all alone, having just lost a baby and with no one by my side. The feeling of emptiness was overwhelming. I cried and cried on the ride over. The cab driver kept asking me if I was okay. I just nodded. It had to be the worst day of my life.

When I arrived at the hospital, I was feeling faint as I had lost a lot of blood. The nurse took me in right away. They admitted me and brought me to a room where they did a curettage (DNC). I stayed overnight after the procedure was finished. I never received a phone call from anyone, including my own husband.

The next day when I arrived home, I walked straight to the bedroom. Ken knew I was mad at him. The two boys were happy to see me and I was happy to see them, but the feeling of hurt and loneliness was so overwhelming that I just crawled into my bed and cried. The boys asked what was wrong and Ken's mother told them everything was going to be all right and she took them out of the room to play with them. Ken looked me right in the face and said he knew I was hurt. He said not to worry and one day we would try again for another baby.

The same night before Ken's mother left, I secretly asked her if she knew if Ken had a girlfriend because she had the number to reach him when he went out and I didn't. She immediately denied the accusation and said Ken would *never* do that to his kids. She said the reason Ken didn't give me the number was that he was afraid I would call too often and bother him at work. (This was not true.) Her words comforted me temporarily, although I knew and felt in my gut this wasn't the case.

One night, it was quite late and our doorbell rang. If I recall correctly, it was approximately 11 p.m. I answered the door to a chubby blond woman who wanted to speak to Ken. The minute Ken heard her voice, he ran to the door. He started yelling at me, saying that I knew the door was for him and to back away from it. He advised the woman that he would be downstairs in a few minutes. She left and closed the door behind her. Ken turned around and took his jacket out of the closet, gathered his keys and left. He didn't say a word to me or the children. I tired peeking out the window but wasn't able to see much. I put the children back to bed and went to lie down myself. Before I knew it I was fast asleep. I couldn't say what time my husband walked back through the door that night.

There was a lot of hatred brewing between Ken and me. His temper was getting worse and worse as time went on. Even though I knew it would stir up a fight, I confronted my husband about the woman at the door. I asked him who she was, I asked him how she knew our address and why she felt the need to show up so late. Ken told me it was Frank's daughter and that she needed money for her sick children. I knew that was a complete lie because Ken had told me years ago that Frank was rich. If this was the case, surely he would help his daughter, wouldn't he? I didn't counter back with anything after that but stored all his lies in the back of my head because, one day, I knew I would find out the truth.

RUMOURS OR TRUTH?

I USED TO VISIT MY MOTHER EVERY OTHER MONTH with the kids. I liked to try and keep in touch and have her spend time with them. The children enjoyed it. While we were talking, my mother quizzed me about Ken. She asked me where he was really going on weekends when he'd tell me he was going to Plattsburgh to buy his porno magazines. And she asked me where I thought he went when he stayed out late every night during the week. I answered to the best of my knowledge from what my husband *told* me about where he was, but the look on my mother's face said she wasn't buying it. She asked me if I was happy, if we were getting along. I told my mother I was lonely and that Ken never wanted to take me anywhere. I didn't tell her about his temper, though; I was afraid of her reaction. My mother tried to convince me that if I wasn't happy, I should file for divorce and make a fresh start. I told her that divorce was out of the question unless I had 100% proof that Ken was indeed cheating on me. My mother then told me to speak with my brothers and sister. Could I? Was this really happening? Would I really let some rumours break my marriage? I didn't have the courage to speak to them, so I made an excuse that I was feeling ill and left with the children soon after.

When I returned home I was so mad that I immediately asked Ken straight out if he had a girlfriend. He looked at me crossly and asked me why I was asking such a question the minute I walked through the door. I told him that my brother had seen him with a woman, and he jumped on me and went for my throat. I was terrified. I was struggling for my life to get away, and he finally let go of me and started smashing and punching all the doors in the house, yelling and screaming and calling me a sick, jealous, ugly bitch. I was scared out of my mind and sorry I had said anything to him in the first place. He had cut up his hands and they were full of blood. He went into the bathroom, yelling, "You see what you did? You see what you did?"

After about a half an hour, he stopped screaming and Ken went to bed in the den area like he always did. It took me a very long time to fall asleep that night because I was quite shaken up from his abusive behaviour.

The next morning I called my mother and told her what happened. I told her Ken was extremely angry at the lies but she insisted they were true. She said my sister Rosie had seen

Ken shopping with a blond woman when he was supposed to be in Plattsburgh. My brother Joe had also seen him with other women. My mother said she wouldn't normally interfere but she knew they were telling the truth and she couldn't just sit back and watch it happen.

That night I begged my husband to tell me the truth. I told him that if he wasn't happy then he could leave and be with whomever it was he wanted to be with and I would take care of the children. I told him I needed to know the truth and that it wasn't fair to the family if he was doing this. My husband looked at me with pure rage in his eyes. He said my family was just as sick as I was. He said that the reason why he was shopping with his old girlfriend (the blond woman) was because he had seen her waiting for the bus on his way to Plattsburgh, and being the gentleman he was, gave her a lift to the grocery store and back home. He said he was going to tell me but he forgot and he didn't think it was such a big deal. Ken said he didn't know why my whole family had sick and twisted minds. He then demanded that I telephone my mother.

My husband forced me, with his gun right next to him, to tell my mother that he was planning on having another private secretary soon and he didn't want any stories getting back to me that he was fooling around. He also made me say that he loved me and that I loved him the same and trusted him completely. He had a speech all written out for me and told me to read it out word for word. He was sitting right in front of me while I was reading this paper to my mother. It broke my heart, but at the same time it was my fear of my husband that led me to do this.

I hung up the phone and started to cry. Ken had a sick grin on his face at this point. He seemed to be enjoying my pain. "That will teach your family to mind their own fucking business," he said. I had no response. I was frozen and felt like a little girl being tortured for no good reason. I couldn't understand why my husband was doing this to me.

I DIVORCE YOU

At this point in our marriage we were having serious financial problems. We needed money. Our bills were backed up and we didn't have enough money to get ourselves out of debt. Ken insisted I ask my father for money. I told him since he was the one taking care of all the bills, he should ask him himself. So he did. One day, he went over to my parents' house and showed my father the inheritance letter from the trust company from Gwen's death. My father believed him when he showed him the letter, so he lent us some money. Ken told my father that when he received the money from the inheritance, he would pay off the mortgage on my parents' house.

A month later, my sister Rose heard about Ken inheriting the money from Gwen's death and showed up at our door asking to borrow money. Ken told my sister that the money was delayed because of tax purposes and that he didn't have any of it yet. My sister was disappointed but, crazily enough, she still believed him.

Three years had passed since Gwen had died and we still hadn't seen any inheritance money. I didn't dare ask Ken about it since he would just insult me and call me a greedy bitch. I wasn't greedy or money-hungry—all I ever wanted was for my husband to treat me like a human being.

Time was passing, the kids were growing and I was becoming lonelier day by day. I used to daydream a lot. My dreams were mostly of having a house in the country. I pictured myself with a lot of children, a house full of colonial furniture, a big backyard and birds singing beautiful songs while I knit outside on the veranda. It was so peaceful: no arguments, no stress, just peace and quiet. I also daydreamed that Ken had changed and he was a kind man who loved me in every way I needed him to. Those daydreams didn't last very long, and when I would come back to reality, I used to cry myself to sleep because I knew our marriage was falling apart and my husband didn't even care. He would tell me that everyone who was married was miserable and we were no different from the rest of society.

Time passed and Ken started bragging about his new secretary, Betty. He would say how beautiful she was and that she had the brains to match. She was efficient and was the perfect match for him in the company. I was told I wasn't allowed to call the office. If I did, I would be disturbing him and he had a lot of work to do to support the family. He would call home occasionally to check on the kids, but it was always a two-minute call—very cold and fast. One night, Ken called to check in and he only asked about Mark. I replied that Mark and Shawn were doing fine and asked him if he was enjoying himself. Ken slammed the telephone in my ear and actually came home early that night. When he walked through the door, very casually I asked him why he was home so early. In a low-toned, vicious-sounding voice, my husband told me if I ever asked him that again he would throw me out of the house without the children. He said he didn't need me and that I was a burden to him. He said there were five to ten women who would love to be with him right now, so I should watch the way I spoke to him. He then said that if I wanted a divorce so badly, he would agree to it and finally be rid of me. What my husband did next was truly unbelievable.

Ken stood in the middle of our bedroom. He spun around three times and yelled out, "I divorce you, I divorce you, I divorce you!" I should have done that years ago!" He was laughing and laughing like he was possessed. I asked him if he really believed we were divorced, and he told me that's the way they did it in certain parts of Africa so it was legal if he wished it to be. I couldn't believe what I was hearing.

Was this really happening? Had my husband completely lost his mind? I told him he could say whatever he wanted but I was still going to a lawyer the next morning. Ken then immediately struck me in the face. He ordered me to shut my mouth and take care of the children. He said if I called the lawyer in the morning he would kill me. He told me that he was doing me a favour by supporting us and I was very ungrateful. I couldn't take his screaming anymore so I ran to the bathroom and turned on the shower to try and block out his screaming.

This started to be a ritual for me. Every time Ken would start his screaming, I would end up in the shower. I tried to do everything and anything to get away from him. It didn't work, though, because at the end of the night when I crept into bed he would start all over again. He seemed to really enjoy yelling at me. The only time my husband would ever be nice to me was when he wanted sex, and that was so rare I couldn't even remember the last time we had been intimate together. I knew my husband had a temper but this was getting way out of control. I had no idea how bad his psychological issues were but it was really starting to affect my well-being. It was horrifying and I saw no way out. I was afraid for my life. I didn't have any friends because Ken wouldn't allow it, so what in the world was I to do?

It was now 1970 and I wanted so badly to have a daughter. It was hard to make this a reality as Ken and I were living like strangers at this point. Things were more peaceful because he would come and go as he pleased; I had long since stopped questioning him about his whereabouts. I didn't want the drama and the abuse so I did everything possible to keep him calm. When I brought up having another child to my husband, he immediately shut me down and said that he only promised me more children because at the time I was depressed.

Money was scarce to none. Ken controlled everything. He never gave me any money to buy clothes and he would always tell me that I didn't need any. Sometimes he would surprise me and buy me an outfit, but I always had to end up scratching his back and combing his hair as a thank you.

I woke up one morning to two bailiffs at my door. I didn't want to open the door but knew I had to. As I slowly cracked it open, they immediately pushed me aside and started taking out our furniture. I started crying and pleading with them to stop until I called Ken at work to ask what was going on, but they just ignored me. They took our TV, stereo and typewriter. They wanted to know if the items belonged to Ken and I told them they did. Before I could make the call to Ken, they were gone. I sat in the house crying. Mark and Shawn just stared at me. They never said a word when these things were happening. I was sure my children were affected by all of this and I prayed and prayed that Ken would change and we could be happy again.

Ken came home later that evening and was furious. He screamed at me so loud I was sure the whole street heard him. I was called every name under the sun. He said I should have lied for him and told the bailiffs that nothing in the house was his. I explained to him that the only reason the bailiffs didn't take everything was that I showed them our marriage contract and they knew I had a right to the other items in the house. He then apologized, but in a sarcastic tone.

Soon after the incident, Ken went to the court to make an application under the Lacombe Law. This was a law that protected your household items if you had gone bankrupt and had no way of paying. There was a fee to pay every month, but this was better than having everything taken away from us.

That month I had missed my menstrual period and was hoping to be pregnant. Ken had taken chances that month, not always using a condom, so there was a possibility. I went to the pharmacy and took a pregnancy test. The minute I found out I was pregnant I told Ken. His reaction was the same, telling me he didn't want another child and that just because I had bionic ovaries didn't mean I had to keep it. He once again demanded I get an abortion. He said he didn't have any patience for another child. I ignored everything he said because there was no way in hell I was getting rid of my baby.

MANIPULATION

IT WAS NOW WINTER OF 1972 AND I WENT TO SEE MY doctor. He confirmed the baby was indeed alive and kicking. I was so happy. I didn't know the sex of the child yet but was secretly hoping for a girl this time.

One night, Ken forced me to telephone his secretary's mother and tell her we were happily married with two children. I made the call out of fear but felt very stupid. He told me his secretary's mother was suspicious that he was having an affair with her daughter because Ken had asked her daughter to become his private secretary at the same time he would have received his inheritance money. It made sense at the time, but this was just another incident that I didn't question because I knew the repercussions that would come from it.

Out of the blue, Ken came home from work one night and started accusing me of sleeping with our milkman. He told me he didn't believe the child I was carrying was his. He grabbed a knife and came at my throat. He started screaming at me to tell him the truth or he would carve the baby out of me. I froze in fear and didn't know what to do. I knew Ken wasn't a drinker, so I thought he was losing his mind. I screamed out in fear, begging him to stop and sit down and talk with me. He did sit down but told me the only reason he didn't kill me was because he needed me to take care of the children. I assured my husband the baby was his and once again cried myself to sleep that night. How could a human being be so cruel?

Springtime came around and Ken advised me he was going to Florida to check on his inheritance. He said he also needed a rest. He told me to make sure I took care of the children and he added in a remark that I was allowed to keep the third baby after all (like it was a privilege). He said that I should be grateful because most men would have forced me have the abortion. I ignored his hurtful remarks and couldn't wait for him to leave so I could be in peace. He said he was tired from working all the time and needed to get away for a while. He said I would never understand because all I did was sit at home with the children and didn't understand the meaning of hard work. The funny thing is Ken didn't want me to work. I was forbidden to work when I started having children with him. To him, a woman's place was the kitchen and the bedroom *only*. He mentioned to me on more than one occasion that there were very few women whom he actually respected.

Ken was all packed for his trip back to Florida. He had packed so much medicine in his suitcase it was unbelievable. Every time Ken would travel he would pack a lot of medicine. You would think he was a doctor. He was paranoid of getting sick or catching any type of disease. His father called to offer him a lift to the airport. Ken refused. I found it very odd but didn't say a word. I knew deep down in my heart that my husband had a mistress; the sad part was that I couldn't prove it.

Once again I was left alone. I kept very busy. Days were spent taking care of Mark and Shawn and nights were filled knitting.

The morning after Ken left, I received a phone call from his boss. He asked to speak with Ken. I was taken aback by this phone call thinking Ken would have advised his boss that he was going away, but I guess I was wrong. I told him Ken would be checking in later on the children and I would have him call him back. Frank then asked me if we were having financial trouble. I told him we were not and asked why he would ask such a question. I was then advised that my husband had defrauded the company for a lot of money and if his boss didn't hear back from him he would be calling the authorities.

I felt quite uneasy about the whole phone call. Why would my husband do this? Where was all the money he took? I had to stop worrying because I didn't want to have another miscarriage.

Ken called to check in on the kids and I told him about what his boss had said. He told me his boss was insane because he had signed a loan already and was starting to pay him back. I didn't know who to believe. Needless to say, I didn't sleep well that night.

Ken cut his trip short. He returned home a couple of days later and advised me that the inheritance was still not settled and that quite a few of Gwen's items were still not sold. He called his boss back, and I overhead them arguing for a very long time. The foul language that came out of my husband's mouth was unbearable. I closed the bedroom door to try and block out all the screaming, but as usual it didn't really help.

What Ken did next was quite disturbing. He called a couple of stores to see if they carried certain types of bullets for guns. Ken owned a shotgun and a rifle as he was a hunter. Every fall was hunting season and Ken would go with a couple of friends to shoot deer. He never actually came home with one, but this was his sport. The odd thing was that the bullets he was looking for were not for his shotgun. He finally found a friend who had the bullets he was looking for. Ken went to get them and came home and starting wrapping them up to go and mail them. I asked Ken why he was doing this and he told me that a friend of his collected them.

Three days later there were detectives at our door. The reason for their visit was to search the house for guns. Ken let them in, and they searched the house and Ken's car. They found Ken's rifle and shotgun but they were not looking for this type of gun, they said. My husband had a licence for his guns so the police couldn't take them away even if they wanted to. After about thirty minutes, they left our home empty-handed. Once the police drove away, my husband started laughing. He bragged about how he had fooled the police. Ken explained how he mailed out the bullets (specifically bullets that did *not* match his guns) out to his enemies to frighten them. He knew the police wouldn't be able to do anything and that thought alone amused Ken. He seems to be enjoying the fact that people were afraid of him and the police didn't have a clue it was him. I was terrified. Why was he doing this?

Out of the blue one day, Ken told me he was getting fed up with living where we were. He didn't like our new landlady and insisted that we look for another to place to live. Our previous landlord had died of a heart attack and the new owners didn't really take a liking to Ken. I thought they were very nice but my opinion was never taken into consideration in our household. All it took was a couple of weeks for Ken to find us another place. It was a lower duplex with a garage. There was a huge playroom for Mark and Shawn and a fenced-off backyard. I was so happy when I saw our new place and couldn't wait for moving day.

Three weeks later, Mark came down with the measles. I called my doctor right away to see how dangerous it was for me since I was pregnant, but my doctor advised me that I was far enough into my pregnancy that neither I, nor the baby, would be affected by this. This was such a relief to me.

THE DISGUISE

KEN WAS A VERY PARANOID HUMAN BEING. HE never understood why I trusted people. He would try and convince me that everyone was against us. He would tell lies about my family and friends to try and turn me against them, but it didn't work. Sometimes I would go along with him for the sake of avoiding an argument, but I knew he was just trying to be controlling. Mind games were his thing, but I didn't have time for any of it. I just wanted to live a normal life, have a loving husband and raise my family. Was this too much to ask?

It was too much to ask and things only became worse. Ken sat me down one evening and told me that we were having serious money problems. He said he had taken a loan from his sister's husband. He didn't tell me the amount, but he did mention that it was a lot. It was from a loan shark at Geza's work. Geza was getting very worried because the loan was overdue and the loan shark was threatening to break his legs if it wasn't paid within forty-eight hours. Geza told Ken on the phone that he had paid it out of fear and that's when my husband blew up! He started screaming at Geza, telling him how stupid he was and that he would never see a cent from Ken.

Ken's sister, Diane, was so upset that her husband had paid the loan and Ken refused to pay him back that she told her father. One evening while we were finishing up supper, Ken's father came over to our home. He came in, played with the kids for a while and then told Ken that he had paid off the loan to Geza and we didn't have anything to stress over now. My husband was so irate at his father that he took him by the arm and escorted him out of the house, screaming at him that he had no right to interfere with our business. Ken's dad was trying to explain that he was only trying to help but Ken kept yelling that he paid the money for nothing because he was going to report the loan shark to the RCMP. The children were quite frightened by Ken's yelling. They both started to cry and then Ken yelled even louder for me to do my job and take them out of the room.

My husband had no respect for anyone or anything. I started to pray nightly to God, asking him to give me the courage to leave this man or show me a way to get him some help. I dreaded when 5 p.m. came around every day because this was the time Ken came home for supper. He would start an argument every single night. It seemed to justify his leaving afterwards.

One afternoon, as I was doing my daily chores, our doorbell rang. I wasn't expecting anyone so this worried me. I went to the door, looked out the peephole, and saw an old man with a cane. I yelled at him that I wasn't interested in what he was selling. As I walked away from the door, the doorbell started ringing and ringing like crazy, and the old man started screaming at me to open the door while calling me a bitch in the process. I was so angry I went back to the door, and as I got closer, I got a better look at the person. It looked an awful lot like Ken. Could it be? Why would he be disguised? What was going on? The man started to press his face against the window to try and look inside and then I realized it was my husband. I immediately opened the door and Ken ran upstairs, throwing away the cane and ripping off his disguise.

What had I just witnessed? What in the hell was going on? I went upstairs after him to ask him why he was disguised as an old man. As I entered the bedroom, he told me not to look at him in that way and yelled that he couldn't even enter his own house without always being questioned. So it would remain a mystery as to why my husband had disguised himself as an elderly man and rung his own doorbell.

A couple of weeks later, the RCMP rang our doorbell. They wanted to ask some questions about Ken. They asked where he worked, how I knew him, what church we were married at, the address of the church and if I was divorced or separated from him. I found the questions odd, so I inquired why they were asking such things. They told me they were verifying some things about Ken and if anything didn't add up, I would be notified by telephone at a later date.

The visit didn't go over well with Ken. He was very upset. Ken was worried because when we had returned from Florida, Ken had flashed his business card at the border patrol to let us get through faster. The business card had the false name Gunfighter Productions, with Ken claiming to be the owner of it.

Lies, lies and more lies. I knew Ken's lies would one day put us in a very difficult position. He never told me about any of his debts until a bailiff came to the door, or we were being sued by creditors. To top it all off, he used to tell me that it was my fault he had the debts in the first place.

I used to check the mail on a daily basis after Ken left for work. One morning I noticed Ken had received mail from a hotel in Montreal. I found the courage to open it, and to my amazement, it was a bill for a two-week stay. I asked my husband about this and he told me that Frank (the man he worked for at night) had lost his credit card and Ken lent him his. Frank's house was being repainted and he needed a place to stay. He told me Frank was good for the money. I knew this was another fabricated story but had no proof so I kept my mouth shut.

Ken always slept in the den. It was like we were not even married anymore. One morning I woke up very dizzy and nauseous. I called out for my husband to help me and he didn't hear me. I couldn't get up so I ended up vomiting on our pale green rug. A few minutes later, he walked into the room screaming at me and calling me a stupid bitch because I ruined the carpet. He immediately ran to get a pail of water and started to clean it. Never once did he ask how I was feeling—all he cared about was getting the rug cleaned. I felt worthless and alone. My own husband didn't care about my well-being, our debts, our happiness or saving our marriage.

Ken called his mother to come over and help me with the boys because I wasn't feeling well. I explained to her the way Ken was behaving, but she didn't say much as she, herself, was afraid of her own son.

BABY #3

FINALLY, IT WAS MOVING DAY! I WAS HAPPY TO BE moving but I won't lie, it was hard, especially with two boys and the fact that I was pregnant again. I knew what it entailed, but not having to climb all those stairs was so worth it. I was, however, realizing more and more each day how horrible of a person my husband really was. He was a rotten father and husband. I was so afraid of him that I tried to find happiness in my children and my hobbies. I felt trapped and alone, so alone. I couldn't find a way out. My husband would continually threaten to kill me and the children if I ever dared to leave him. He made it clear on almost a daily basis. I was so brainwashed that I could never see a way out.

The movers did a great job for us. I needed help, though, to push the boxes into each of the rooms. Ken refused to help me, saying that he had to go back to the old house to get his pornographic magazines. Ken had hundreds and hundreds of them. It literally took him all night until 4 a.m. the next morning to transfer all of them to our new place.

Our boys made friends quite quickly. The mother of the children from next door came by to introduce herself. She was very nice and her children were all well behaved. I liked her so much that I invited her back another time to have coffee. I told Ken about the nice neighbours next door. Ken was not impressed by them and told me that I was forbidden to speak with them and threatened to kill me if I ever told anyone about his business. I couldn't believe what I heard. I was happy and so were the children. It seemed he tried to destroy any type of happiness in our household altogether.

The year was 1971. I was swollen as hell—about eight months pregnant and summer was nearly over. I was expecting my third child and my son Shawn was starting kindergarten that year. It was now the end of August, and the cooler weather was starting to approach. That was a relief for me as the doctor had advised me to stay off my feet as much as I could because phlebitis was starting to set in. My husband didn't care. He kept going out every single night after work and leaving me to tend to Mark and Shawn alone.

I started to notice a change in behaviour from Ken. He started bringing home gifts; he also brought home outfits for the boys and purchased new furniture for the house. I asked him where all of this money was coming from and he told me he'd started to receive some of Gwen's inheritance.

Did we finally have a degree of financial freedom? Did Ken actually get some inheritance money? I wanted to believe my husband, but at the same time it was next to impossible to do this.

As time passed, I started seeing less and less of my husband. The house was so quiet and peaceful. It felt nice not having to be on edge all the time. I wished my marriage would take a turn for the better, but having to be realistic, I knew that it was never going to happen.

September came and I was in my last month of pregnancy. I was still taking the boys to school every morning. The daily walk did me some good and I was able to reflect on my life at this time. Shawn didn't particularly like kindergarten. I remember one morning when he was just about to enter the school, he started crying and refusing to go inside. I asked him what the problem was and he didn't answer me. Thankfully, there was a school nurse named Brenda who had her daughter in the same class. She took Shawn by the hand and went inside with him. When I looked through the classroom window, I saw Shawn playing calmly with her daughter and felt grateful she was able to calm him down. We ended up becoming good friends as she lived just a street away from us. I couldn't tell Ken, though, as he didn't want me having any friends at all.

September 24th came around and my labour started. It was early morning and I told Ken. He immediately called his mother to come and look after Mark and Shawn. While we were in the waiting room at the hospital, I was getting so aggravated with Ken. No woman wants their husband telling them *when* to give birth. He was trying to rush my labour, saying that he had to get back to the office to do the payroll for the employees. He didn't give a fig about me, the new baby, my pain or suffering. He was simply a selfish man, and once again it broke my heart. This behaviour lasted for about five hours and then finally the baby was ready to come out. When Ken found this out he yelled loudly, "Yes! I can finally go do the payroll!"

My third baby was another beautiful baby boy! He weighed nine pounds, one ounce. I decided to name him Wayne. I now had three boys. What a nice little family. I was once again on cloud nine. My husband only came to visit me once in the hospital. He only wanted to show the baby off to his parents.

After a couple of days I was discharged from the hospital. Ken said that he would come to get us and to make sure I was ready when he came. I was in the process of slowly getting ready when Ken arrived. He asked me where the baby was and I told him that the nurse didn't bring Wayne as of yet. I told him to sit down and relax for a couple of minutes. He insisted on pacing back and forth, telling me to hurry up. Again, I told him to sit and relax for a couple of minutes and he yelled at me to shut my mouth. He then left the room to go and look for the nurse. A couple of minutes later, Ken came back with the nurse and Wayne. We started to get Wayne dressed. The nurse helped me as I was always a little nervous with my newborns. Ken rushed the nurse, as well, telling her to hurry up and that everyone in the hospital was so slow. She then turn to him and said that the hospital's policy was to have me wheeled out in a wheelchair. Ken left the room with the baby and told the nurse to wheel me out.

I started to cry. The nurse felt sorry for me. She asked me if my husband was suffering from a nervous breakdown. I asked her why she would ask such a question. She told me never in her twenty years of working at the hospital she had never heard someone speak to his wife that way and want to rush her out after giving birth.

We left the hospital and made our way home. As soon as we walked through the front door, Ken handed Wayne to his mother and off he went. He yelled out that he had to rush to court for an appointment and he would be home by dinner time. He said there was a misunderstanding that he had to straighten out. So much for going back to work and doing the payroll, I guess.

Dinner time passed and Ken had not returned. I fed the children and put them to bed. I sat there on the couch with my newborn baby and two other children and no husband around. I knew Ken wasn't invested in our family but I always had hope. Hope that he would change, want to love me, want to love the children and show them what it was like to be a man. Instead, my husband had this secret life that neither I, nor anyone else, knew anything about. I wanted to know the truth, wanted to know so badly, yet at the same time, I was terrified of him and knowing the truth.

It was now nearly 11 p.m. I heard the phone ring and answered it immediately so the boys would not wake up. It was Ken. He was calling from jail. He told me that some judge who thought he was God put him there. I almost collapsed with disbelief. He gave me three different lawyers' numbers to call. I tried all three and got an answering machine each time, asking me to call back Monday morning.

I panicked, so I called the jail. I had only seen movies about people in jail so I was under the impression they were only fed bread and water. I spoke with the guard and asked him if my husband was being fed. He laughed at me and said that Ken was only in a holding centre and, yes, of course he was being fed. He told me that it wasn't a hotel but he had his meals and was just fine. This relieved me and I was able to sleep a little better that night.

Monday morning came and Ken appeared in court. He got bail. Once he got home he finally told me what was going on. He said that the bank had charged him with fraud and that the court date was a preliminary hearing. He told me he pleaded not guilty but the judge apparently found him very rude and gave him three days in jail in a holding cell at a prison called Parthenais. The fraud charge originated from Peter, Ken's old boss. I then recalled the telephone call I had received from Peter a couple of years back, asking why Ken wasn't at work. Peter had told me that Ken had cashed a bank draft belonging to the company.

Now I was extremely worried. What kind of future was I heading into with such a secretive, dishonest and cruel man? My heart wanted so badly to believe my husband; I wanted to forget all the bad things he had done, but at the same time I was so terrified that if I left him, he would kill all of us that my idea of starting a new life shattered quite quickly.

Ken kept postponing the court date. He was told by his lawyer that the longer he stalled, the better chance he had at winning the case.

We had long nights with Wayne. Out all of the babies, he was the fussiest. Wayne was always hungry. For the first year he used to wake up every night, screaming for another bottle of milk. He made Ken so nervous when he cried that Ken used to curse at him. He would call him a "fucking little bastard." Ken used to say that he was lucky that he allowed him to live and now he wouldn't even let him sleep. He was furious at the fact that Wayne was crying and it was disturbing him. He said his son was an evil curse and that it was his fault he got arrested. He made this assumption because the day Ken was arrested was the night Wayne was born.

Something was definitely wrong with my husband. He was really starting to hate Wayne and this frightened me terribly. My husband was experiencing a serious change in his behaviour. On weekdays, he started coming home at lunchtime. He would take out his typewriter and start writing cheques. He never ate and always made an excuse that he was in a rush. Suppertime would come around and he would eat so fast that by the time I made my own plate, he would already be done and have left the table. He would also start an argument with me most nights (especially on the nights he would go out), which was practically every other night.

Our lovemaking had just about stopped. Ken became very heavy, weighing over 300 pounds. He was very insecure about his weight; he was too heavy to fit in the bathtub so he used to wash with a facecloth only. His hair was so filthy it smelled of grease a mile away. I tried to convince him to clean himself regularly, but every time I did he would just insult me.

At this time I was thirty-one and Ken was thirty-seven. Wayne was about seven months old at the time. Mark was seven and Shawn was five. One night, Ken wanted to get frisky. I wasn't really in the mood but gave in anyway. Yes, you can imagine what came out of that. I found out I was pregnant, once again! I was thrilled, as my children were my only reason for existing at this point.

THE BLOODIED COAT

IT WAS NOT THE IDEAL SITUATION INTO WHICH TO bring a fourth child. Ken and I barely even spoke and, as always, he was extremely distant. My intuition told me that he had another woman on the side and I didn't care. Well, at least, that's what I told myself. I knew that, in time, I would find evidence of this, and then I would have a reason to divorce him.

I started knitting pretty little pink dresses in hopes for a girl this time. My children fulfilled me almost completely. What I was lacking was love from my husband. I felt so empty inside. The joke of it all was that I was actually willing to spend the rest of my life with Ken if he was willing to change. I used to pray on a daily basis that he would change for the better, but instead Ken was getting more and more abusive, both mentally and physically. He never smoked or drank a day in his life; his bad habit was tranquilizers. He used to take Valium daily.

My fourth pregnancy wasn't an easy one. At six months in, my legs, feet and hands were extremely swollen. I had to lower my salt intake and rest more often. The salt part wasn't an issue, but resting with three young children was practically impossible.

My husband was up to something. Most nights, he would make telephone calls late at night on the second telephone line he had installed—without telling me why. I wasn't *ever* allowed to answer the second line, even if it rang all night.

One evening, my brother Joe telephoned Ken. Once the call ended, Ken started yelling that Joe had let him down. He then mumbled something under his breath. I didn't catch everything he was saying, but it sounded as if he was planning to do some harm to my brother. I told Ken to try and calm down and control himself. He then started cursing even more, punching all the walls in the house. I couldn't calm him down, nor did I really try. I went to bed, hoping that my husband would be in a better mood before he went to sleep. I had fallen asleep when he came in but was awakened by Ken's hand on my belly. He touched it very softly and spoke to the baby, saying how much he loved it. We didn't know yet if it was a boy or a girl, as I always wanted it to be a surprise. I found it very creepy when he did that. I knew something was wrong for sure. Every single pregnancy before this one, he'd wanted me to have an abortion, and now he was saying he loved the baby? I just smiled at him and didn't say a word.

The next day Ken left for work as usual. About half an hour later the doorbell rang. I was still half asleep, so it took me a while to get to the door. I heard Ken screaming for me to open the door and calling me a stupid bitch for not getting to the door fast enough. Once I opened the door, he pushed me aside and ran straight to the bathroom. His coat was totally drenched in blood! I was so stunned and paralyzed by what I was seeing that I couldn't even speak. He grabbed a suitcase and threw in a bunch of clothes, telling me he was in trouble and was on his way to Plattsburgh.

He was moving so fast I didn't even have a chance to say a word. My heart was racing and I was feeling very light-headed, as if I was going to collapse. I watched him change his clothes, put the bloodied coat in the garbage, pack his suitcase and make a phone call to his friend. I had the courage to finally ask him if he'd murdered someone. He looked at me with disgust and yelled that he didn't but that what just went down was all my brother's fault. He said that everyone in my family was stupid, including myself. His eyes were dark. My husband was terrified. I had never seen him like this before. He ordered me to hide the typewriter in the hamper and to put it in the closet. I did exactly as he asked. He then ran out the door telling me the police would be there soon and to tell them I hadn't seen him since last night. He said he would contact me from Plattsburgh when he could.

Once he shut the door I fell to the floor with grief. I cried and cried for hours. What had just happened? Did my husband kill someone? What should I tell the police?

I was so scared I must have drunk six cups of coffee and smoked half a pack of cigarettes. Ken was right: the police showed up not too long after. They rang the bell. Outside were two police cars. Here I was, alone with three children and pregnant with my fourth. I went to the door. The police identified themselves and asked to come in.

They asked if Ken lived there. I told them, yes, he did, but that he was currently at work. They started searching the house as if they were looking for him. They didn't say a word, just kept searching. They entered Wayne's room, where he was sleeping, and immediately woke him up. He started to cry. They proceeded downstairs to the basement part of our house. A couple of minutes later, the officer came upstairs with handcuffs and Ken's hunting supplies. They asked me about them. I told him I didn't even know he had them. Ken never wanted me to know anything about his life. He dangled the cuffs in front of me and said, "Lady, be very careful because any man who owns handcuffs and is not a police officer, to me, is a very cruel man." He then gave me his card and told me to call him once I heard from Ken. They left right after that.

I pondered his words over the next few days. What could the police officer have meant by that? What was Ken planning on doing with handcuffs anyway?

I didn't do much around the house that morning. Ken called me about an hour after the police had left. He wanted to know every detail about what they searched and what exact questions they asked. He never once asked how I was feeling or how the children were. He told me he was in Plattsburgh and that he had to get things straightened out before he came back. I started crying on the telephone, telling him I had no money and wasn't able to feed the children. Ken then said he was going to call my brother Richard and ask him to lend us some money.

When the phone call ended I burst into tears. I had to get it together. I didn't want to lose the baby because of my nerves, and the boys would be coming home soon from school for lunch. I took a quick shower and tried to pull myself together.

The boys came home for lunch but I didn't say a word to them. I didn't have the heart to tell them their father was on the run from the police. I acted as normal as I could, fed them lunch, and then they went back to school. I called my mother after the children left. I told her that Ken was in serious trouble and I didn't know what to do. She had a lot of questions as to what kind of trouble. I told her I didn't know the whole story and couldn't give her the answers she wanted. Never once did she offer me any help or sympathize with me. I hung up and tried to figure out a way to get some money for the kids. I called the welfare office in our area and told them that my husband deserted me, we had three children and I was six months pregnant. I told them I had no money for food and was desperate for help. They took my name and telephone number and advised me that someone would come to the house the next day to assess my situation. This made me feel a little less stressed.

I didn't sleep well that night, let me tell you. Early the next morning, my doorbell rang. It rang and rang like someone had their hand on the bell and wouldn't let go. I rushed to the door as fast as I could and saw it was the police. I opened the door and they pushed right past me, flashing a paper in my face stating they had a warrant out for Ken's arrest and wanted to know where he was. They searched the house up and down. I asked them what my husband had done and they didn't have any answers for me. All they said was there was a warrant out for his arrest. I told them I had no idea where he was and couldn't help them. This time they were extra nice, asking me how our children were and how I was feeling. I'm sure they were also questioning the neighbours as to Ken's whereabouts.

The police left and then a representative from the welfare office came that afternoon. I told them my story about how I was alone with the children and had a fourth child on the way. They were very nice and helpful. They immediately gave me welfare. They also advised me to move into a smaller place because of the fact that the money they were providing would only cover the rent.

THE SEARCHES

IF ANYONE NEEDED A MIRACLE AT THIS TIME IT WAS me. Life seemed to be at its worst for me. I prayed and prayed to God to guide me in the right direction. I wished I had never married this man and that this wasn't happening to me. What had I done to deserve this? My faith in God was starting to diminish as more and more negativity entered my life.

Ken called the house later on that night on our second telephone. We had two telephones in the house. One was upstairs and one was in the basement. The telephone in the basement was an unlisted number and therefore could not be traced by the police. This was the phone he always called home on. I asked my husband what he had done that was so bad it could warrant an arrest by the police. I needed to know. I needed to know the truth even if I didn't like the answer I was going to hear.

Ken told me that he and his friend Alfie had gone over to his boss's house to make him sign a paper stating that Ken never committed any fraud to his company. Ken had gotten fired because of this accusation. He was prolonging the court date for months now and needed his boss to sign the paper to prove he didn't do it, otherwise he knew he could be convicted and probably serve time in jail for this. Ken then told me that everything had gone wrong. He said his boss had a head injury, they had to leave the apartment in a rush, and that this was the reason for the blood on his coat. My husband didn't go into further detail, and I didn't dare to ask. I was never told who was actually responsible for his boss's head injury.

Ken told me that when he left his boss's apartment, he also left his briefcase behind. Inside the briefcase were items that could possibly convict him. There was an unsigned check of Ken's that he was planning on forcing his boss to sign to give him money. In my husband's mind, his boss owed him money because of the fact that he was lying about him committing fraud. He thought that he owed him, and this was his way of telling the truth—his way of getting back at him.

Two weeks went by and during this time the police would randomly check the house every two or three days at different times of the day to see if Ken was there. I had absolutely no privacy. Thank goodness the checks were always during the day and the boys were at school, but it still took a toll on me. I was a nervous wreck. I couldn't eat and I couldn't sleep.

The visits from the police were less frequent after the first two weeks, but they were still very unsettling. They would always arrive without notice, always at different times of the day, and search the house in a rough and rude manner.

We had a milkman who used to come once a week in our area. This was very convenient as I had the children and it wasn't always easy to get out to the store. One morning he passed by and rang the bell. I found this odd as he usually just left the milk in the front of the house. I answered the door and to my surprise he was standing there with a huge smile on his face. He asked me how I was feeling and told me how beautiful I was. He then proceeded to tell me that Ken was crazy to leave me and he actually leaned over to try and kiss me! I pushed him away and was so frazzled I almost tripped over the front stairs. What nerve! I couldn't believe what had just happened. I was seven months pregnant and showing a lot. Didn't he know this? Had he no respect?

I wasn't going to lie to myself, though. I did like the attention and was very flattered at the same time. My husband never gave me any attention so any attention I received from *any* man was flattering.

My friend Bertha starting stopping by more often for coffee since I was alone every day. It was great company when the kids were in school. Since Ken was away in Plattsburgh, I was able to have more freedom to speak to my friends without an argument from Ken. I felt that, deep down, they knew something was going on, but they never said a word. I found myself telling lie after lie when it came to questions about Ken. I think the only people who really knew what was going on were Ken's parents and his lawyer.

A couple of days later, my brother Richard showed up at the door. He said Ken called him and asked him for a personal loan for us. My brother then asked if I was going to join Ken in Plattsburgh any time soon. I told him I didn't think I was going to as I had too much going on at home with the children. He stayed for a while, played with the kids after they came home from school, and left shortly after that. It was nice to see my brother. I missed my family terribly.

I started spotting blood off and on because of the stress I was going through. Dr. Bailey told me to relax more, and at one point he gave me some meds to calm me down, which were not harmful to the baby. I mentioned to Dr. Bailey that I might join Ken down in the US if it was his plan to stay there. The doctor advised against it, saying if Ken really loved me he would come back and face whatever was going on. He said I was at risk to lose the baby if I kept on stressing about the situation. I liked this about Dr. Bailey; he always listened to me. He never rushed me out of his office and always gave me his personal opinion. Dr. Bailey was the only person I told about my life with Ken. He felt sorry for me and always tried to help me. It was reassuring and I felt I was in good hands with this doctor.

Ken called one morning and asked to see the boys. He said his parents would drive us down to Plattsburgh. I didn't feel like going as I was exhausted from taking care of the children and being seven months pregnant, but I packed the suitcases and went anyway.

DECISIONS

WE ARRIVED A LITTLE BEFORE DINNER TIME. KEN met us outside the motel. He brought the suitcases up to the room. He didn't pay any attention to me at all, ask how I was doing or say that he missed me. He was just concerned about the clothes I brought for him. I cleaned the boys up and they ate supper and I put them to bed. Ken stayed in the room with the boys for a bit and then told his mother and me to go downstairs to the restaurant to eat.

Ken's mother knew I was hurting from the way her son was ignoring me. I could see it in her eyes. I was starving. At the restaurant I ordered a steak with all the trimmings. I didn't care how expensive it was. The least my husband could do for me was feed me properly. I knew he wanted us out of the motel room so he could talk with his dad. The food was good that night and I couldn't wait to get back to the room to get some rest.

We went back to the room about an hour later. The children were fast asleep. Ken's parents had an adjacent room to ours. Ken asked if we could all meet in the living room so we could talk. I couldn't have been more excited to hear what was going to come out of my husband's mouth. I suggested that we talk alone in private, but my husband insisted that he had nothing to hide from his parents and wanted all of us in on the conversation.

So, into the living room we went. Ken asked us all to sit. He then stood up in front of me and asked me and the children to leave with him in the morning as he was planning to move to Florida. I couldn't believe what I was hearing. I explained to Ken that the doctor advised me not to travel as I was at risk of having a miscarriage. The boys were in school and I couldn't just pick up and leave. What the hell was he thinking? His father interrupted and said that the children would adjust and if I loved him I would go with him. His mother, on the other hand, had more sense. She said if and when I had the baby and more money, then and only then should I go and make a life with Ken in Florida. The conversation ended quite abruptly when I declined to go Florida with my husband. Ken stormed off into the bedroom, yelling that his father was the only one who loved and understood him.

I was so sorry I made the trip to Plattsburgh. Sleeping that night was next to impossible. Besides the fact that my husband was snoring loudly in my ear, I had stomach cramps from all the stress, and the kids were waking up every two hours for attention. There was absolutely no reason for me to be there with him. I cried and cried myself to sleep that night.

The next morning, Ken woke up early and told everyone he was leaving for Florida. He told me to go home with the children. He let his father know that he would be calling from time to time, but not often, as long distance calls were very expensive and he didn't have the money to do so. His father said not to worry about calling because all he had to do was reverse the charges and he would pay for it. Ken coldly said goodbye to the children and absolutely not a word to me. He pretended I wasn't even there. The ride back to Montreal with Ken's parents was a quiet one. No one said much in the car that day.

It was December 1972, and I was still in my seventh month of pregnancy. My legs, feet and ankles were very swollen. I was exhausted and the children were always so active. This was a real challenge for me. I loved my children but I must admit I was tired.

I called my mother one day and told her the whole story. I know she felt bad for me. She gave me some advice and kept reminding me that I had to think of the baby coming and forget about Ken's negativity. She said that maybe Ken would do well in Florida and send for me. Send for me? Was this what I wanted? I was so confused and had so many mixed emotions I didn't know what to think.

Sooner than later, the inevitable happened. My husband finally called me. He told me that he was able to get his friend Alfie to accompany him on his trip to Florida. He said he was staying at the Playboy Hotel and kept bragging about how nice the weather was and how much fun he was having. He did mention that he was sorry for the way he left but not once did he say that he missed or loved me or the children. I asked him if he was job hunting and he told me he was waiting for his papers to be fixed. I knew that meant a big fat *no*. Alfie stayed for two weeks and then flew back home to Montreal. He had a wife, children and a job, so he couldn't stay in Florida like Ken did.

I was now nearing the end of my eighth month of pregnancy. I had gained a lot of weight and had a lot of trouble getting around, especially to run errands. Ken's father would take me to do the groceries when I needed. I was happy he did, but he drove me insane. He would put junk food in the cart that I didn't need, was loud in the store and could never ever find his car after we were done. I was so fed up with him that I started taking taxis instead when I had to get groceries.

One morning I received a call from Ken's insurance broker, Jack. He started asking me questions about Ken. They were very personal questions. Jack was also a friend of ours. He told me that Ken had called him from Miami asking to borrow money. He said that if Jack didn't lend him any money, he would commit suicide. Jack was trying to figure out if Ken had gambling issues or was maybe linked in some way to the Mafia. Jack told me that he himself didn't have much money and couldn't lend him more than thirty or forty dollars. He was scared for Ken, though. He wanted to call the Miami police to report a possible suicide attempt. I had a very long conversation with Jack and convinced him that my husband was just down and he would never do that to himself or our family. I would say it took about two hours to convince Jack not to call the police. When I hung up the phone with Jack, I was so angry. Not too long after, Ken called me to tell me how much of an asshole Jack was because he wasn't lending him any money. He told me how he tried to trick Jack into lending him money by stating that he would commit suicide but it didn't work. He didn't even care how upset it made Jack or me that he was doing this. All he cared about was trying to get some money. I listened to my husband on the phone, not saying much, but told myself enough is enough. When I hung up the phone, I called the operator to tell her not to put any more calls through collect that came from Ken's number in Florida because I couldn't afford them anymore. I couldn't handle his behaviour. It was draining and consuming all of my happiness towards the children. I had three children and one more on the way to care for, and my husband wasn't making my life any easier.

It was now close to Christmas and Ken's mother bought me a colonial-style cradle. It was beautiful! I had always wanted one for my babies and I finally got one. I set it up with all the bedding and some stuffed animals in the corner. The cradle was nicely done up in pastel colours. I was really hoping for a girl this time. I kept it neutral, though, with pastel greens and yellows.

The landlord passed by a few days later to collect December's rent. It was usually Ken who gave it to him, so I knew when I answered the door he was probably going to ask where he was. I was sure all the neighbours had told him that Ken was on the run from the police. I dreaded answering the door to the multiple questions he would have. I was embarrassed and quite nervous at the same time. To my surprise, he didn't ask about Ken. He did, however, tell me that my eyes looked sad and that meant I was having a girl. He also asked if I was going to renew the lease in the summer. I told him I was going to have to move in May. It broke my heart to tell him but I just couldn't afford to live there anymore. It was the perfect house, the children had the big backyard and the playroom in the basement. I had to stop living beyond my means and face the reality that my husband was on the run from the police and I was alone with three children and could barely survive financially on welfare. I paid the landlord the rent, and after a ten-minute chat, he was on his way.

Ken's mother telephoned me a few days before Christmas. She told me that Ken was now in Plattsburgh (he had left Florida), and wanted to see the boys. She knew Ken and I were not on talking terms and offered to take the boys down there for me. I told her that if they were to go I would be accompanying them, as well. There was no way I was going to let her take my boys alone. She agreed and off we went.

The boys were happy to see their dad. That part of the visit went well. We did a bit of shopping and the kids had fun at the hotel pool. Ken's parents paid for the hotel and all of the meals. When it came time to sleep, Ken told me to sleep with Wayne and he took the other bed with Shawn and Mark. He barely said two words to me, and when he did look at me, he looked at me with disgust. I knew something was wrong. This was not a normal way for a husband to be towards his wife. He never once asked me how I was, how the baby was doing, or said that he missed or loved me. All I did was support him, stay home and take care of the children, and this was the gratitude he gave in return?

It was Christmas Eve and we drove back to Montreal. Ken's mother cried when we left. She didn't want to leave Ken in the hotel. Yes, she cried, for a grown man who treated us like garbage. Ken's father made Ken promise he would call his mother every day. They were treating him like a child. He was a grown man and wasn't able to face the music by coming home and giving himself up to the police. There was a warrant out for his arrest and his parents just pretended nothing was going on. They would just give him money and pray he was safe.

We spent Christmas of 1972 alone. Ken apparently drove back to Florida and was having a good old time doing God knows what. My eldest son Mark asked me that day about his father. Mark was nine years old at the time and very intelligent. He asked if his dad was somehow in trouble with the police. I was taken aback by the question and asked him why he would ask that. He told me that he'd overheard (though he didn't tell me where) that his dad had to straighten something out and then was going to finally move to Florida. Mark asked me if we could all move down there. I told him it was up to his father and we would have to wait to see what happened. Who was I fooling? We were never going to move to Florida. We were never going to live as a happy, loving family. These thoughts completely consumed me and I went into my bedroom and quietly cried for the next twenty minutes. I heard a knock at the door and it was my son Shawn. He asked if I was all right since I had the door closed and usually never did. I immediately wiped my face and told him I was and that I would be out in a minute. At this moment, I knew my husband was poison to our family. It was getting to me. It was bringing me down. I didn't want our children to feel the pain I felt. I didn't want the children to know their father was a failure. That he was a cruel and distant man. I just wanted everything to go away. I opened the bedroom door and told Shawn everything was fine and went to the basement and played some board games with them. They opened their gifts, which were mostly bought buy Ken's parents. I made sure to buy a few small presents throughout the year—with the help of my mother—to ensure that they all had a little something under the tree. It was nice; a nice quiet night. Even though Christmas was very peaceful, I still missed my husband, I felt bad for the children, as well. But it was what it was, and I needed to find a way to make it better.

FLORIDA

New Year's came and went. Winter that year was pretty brutal. The cold temperatures aggravated the arthritis in my back and made it painful. It was now mid-January and the baby was due in a few weeks. I was getting quite excited.

I received a phone call from Ken while he was in Plattsburgh. He was crying on the phone and asked me if he went to jail, would I wait for him. He said he was going to finally turn himself in. I told him I would wait if he was man enough to do that. Ken then made a plan. He said we would meet at his parents' place and go together to the lawyer's office. I couldn't believe my husband was asking me to do this while I was in my last stage of pregnancy. Getting me involved in all of his problems and his wrongdoings. He made me sick, but I did it anyway.

Once we were at the lawyer's office, Ken asked the lawyer to tell me how much time he would be facing if he was convicted of the fraud charge he had hanging over him. I was told two to twenty years depending on if the judge was strict or not. Ken got up from his chair and left the office at that point. He left me sitting in the lawyer's office alone. I apologized on his behalf and thanked the lawyer for his time.

I walked back to the car, infuriated, ready to blast my husband for leaving me alone in the lawyer's office, and as soon as I opened the car door—to my surprise—I saw my husband weeping like a child. He kept sobbing and sobbing. He said he tried to give himself up but he couldn't stand being in jail for one day, never mind twenty years.

It all felt like a dream. Was this being staged? Did Ken make all of this up? When we arrived home, Ken asked me if he could take Mark and Shawn to Florida. I wasn't too pleased at this idea. I knew damn well the judge wouldn't have given him twenty years on his first fraud charge, let alone, when did he have any interest in bringing the kids anywhere? Ken's mother was in on it, as well. She told me that Wayne was more than enough for her to handle when I went to the hospital to have the baby. She tried to coax me into letting Ken take the two older boys on a mini vacation. Something just wasn't right.

My husband was the type of man who needed a woman around to do everything for him. This idea of his was very fishy. Did he have another woman down in Florida? Could that be possible? Before I could even give him an answer, Ken blurted out to Mark and Shawn that he was taking them to Florida so I could rest before the baby came. The boys cheered with excitement! I had never seen them so happy. I agreed, but on one condition: that once the baby was born, Ken would return with the boys. Ken agreed and asked me for their birth certificates. I found that quite odd as he was only going for a week or so, so I refused to give them to him.

The next day Ken left with the boys. I packed the car and gave Mark and Shawn big hugs and kisses. They were so excited for their trip with their dad. Ken didn't even say goodbye to me. He hugged Wayne and then drove off like I didn't even exist. I cried inside—I cried so hard. My two oldest boys were gone and I should have been happy to have the time to rest, but all I felt was emptiness inside. My husband didn't love me anymore and I knew it. Our marriage was failing and I could not do a thing about it.

Days passed and I didn't receive a phone call or an update on the boys. Finally Ken's mother came to tell me that Ken called her and told her everything was fine with the boys. Why wasn't he calling me? Why was he going through his mother? I knew something wasn't right but I didn't have any proof of anything. It killed me inside, knowing my husband was being deceitful in some way, but I couldn't wrap my thoughts around it. I just couldn't.

It was January 29th and my labour pains started. I called Ken's mother so she could be ready to take Wayne when I had to go to the hospital. Wayne was well behaved and he enjoyed being with his grandmother. He was sixteen months old now and never gave her a hard time. While I was packing my bag, I heard Ken's mother call Ken on our phone. Wait—she knew his phone number and never gave it to me? I was so hurt but pretended not to be bothered by it. She passed the phone over to me and Ken apologized for not being able to make it to the hospital and that he would be home soon. Small talk as usual.

Off to the hospital I went. Ken's Aunt Ethel drove me there. She stayed, as well. I liked Aunt Ethel. She was down to earth, knew what Ken was all about and felt sorry for me. She wouldn't sugar-coat anything, yet in the same breath she would always tell me that things have a way of working themselves out and to have faith. I wasn't sure what she meant by that but enjoyed her company nevertheless. After the doctor checked me, my labour pains subsided. The pain was tolerable at this point. I was told to rest and I did exactly that. Aunt Ethel read her book and I fell asleep.

At 11:45 p.m. that evening, I awoke to excruciating labour pains. Aunt Ethel tried to calm me down but nothing worked.

The baby was coming and coming fast! I rang the nurse's bell. In came a young nurse. She seemed quite nervous. She checked me and told me she saw the tip of the baby's head. She begged me not to push and said that she was getting the doctor right away.

Within minutes I was wheeled into the delivery room. Dr. Shams was there and ready to deliver the baby. He looked at me and shouted, "Okay, Mrs. Robinson, one big push and you're done!" To my surprise, that's exactly what it took. Fifteen minutes of labour and I was looking at my beautiful baby girl! I couldn't believe it. She was born at the stroke of midnight. The doctor put her on my stomach, and I had to look at her to make sure she was, indeed, a girl. Having three boys already it was hard to believe I finally had my daughter. She was perfect in every way. I decided to name her Wendy. Dr. Shams went into the hallway to tell Ethel the good news. She was thrilled for me.

The next morning the telephone rang in hospital room. It was Ken from Florida. He called to congratulate me on our baby girl. I asked him if he was happy to finally have a girl, and he said as long as I was happy that was all that mattered. I asked to speak to the boys and he said they were busy playing outside. I was crushed. Again, no emotion whatsoever from my own husband. Tears fell down my cheeks once again. This was supposed to be one of the happiest days of my life, yet I was so emotionally drained by the fact that my husband couldn't care less about his family. He sucked the joy right out of my body. A thought crossed my mind. Maybe he did miss me but couldn't show it because he was nervous about his court case coming up? Was there still hope? Could we still make it work?

Ethel stayed at our house for a couple of days to help with Wayne and the baby. It felt really nice to have some help. Wayne loved his little sister.

Ken drove back from Florida about a week later with Mark and Shawn. He was so paranoid that a neighbour would call the police on him if they saw him because he still had the outstanding warrant from his fraud charge. So he drove straight to his parents' place with the boys. They went inside and went straight to bed. Ken's mother called me to let me know they arrived safe and said she would bring them home in the morning.

I couldn't sleep that night. I knew he was wanted by the police, but who didn't bring their children home right away? What kind of a monster was he?

Ken's dad brought Mark and Shawn home the next morning. They were very excited to see their new baby sister, Wendy. It felt good for all the children to be back together. The boys were very gentle around her and enjoyed their time together. It helped that they were being so good because I was exhausted and still bleeding very heavily for some reason after giving birth to her.

Ken's mother called a couple of days later and told me Ken had driven back to Florida. She was happy and said Ken was now free! His parents paid for all his trips; in fact, they even took out personal loans to do so. I couldn't believe it. I had just given birth to our fourth child, my husband was on the run from the police, he didn't even make an effort to come and see our daughter when she was born, and now he was back in Florida? My emotions were running high and my patience was running thin.

THE MOVE

I WAS PREPARING FOR WENDY'S BAPTISM. I HAD asked my brother Joe to be the godfather and my sister Linda to be the godmother. They both agreed. On the day of the baptism, the priest gave a special blessing. At the church there were always multiple baptisms going on at the same time. All the proud fathers gathered together and held the candles, while the mothers held the babies. The priest noticed that I was alone with my baby. He immediately asked my brother Joe to stand next to me with the candle. He said even the godfathers need a blessing. Everyone chuckled; everyone but me. I cried inside. I was broken.

After the church ceremony, we all went back to my house for refreshments and a nice meal. My dad knew I was upset and brought me into the bedroom to have a talk. He asked me what was going on. He knew I wasn't happy and hadn't been for a long time at that. He told me that if I wasn't going to join Ken down in Florida then I should file for divorce because it was not healthy for the children or me being this way. He said I was only thirty-two and still young enough to start over again. I heard him. I heard all his wise words but didn't know if I was strong enough to put them into action.

I left the bedroom after my father did. I'll do it, I said to myself. I'll move to Florida. What could I lose? I was miserable living like this anyway—alone, lonely and not knowing what was going on. I exited the bedroom and announced to my family the plan of action I was going to take. I told them that maybe Ken had changed and I was going to move to Florida so we could raise the children together as a family. Everyone was pleased. I even heard someone say in the background that children needed both parents to be raised properly. Wow! Where would I start? I had so much to sell!

My in-laws were shocked at my news. They said I should have told Ken my decision before announcing it to my family. Ken's mother said there wasn't any Medicare in Florida and didn't know if my decision would be the best one for the family. I thought this was so hypocritical, as the whole time we were in Plattsburgh, she had been telling me that a wife belongs with her husband, but now her opinion had changed.

Nevertheless, I started selling items from around the house. Within a week, the news that I was moving had spread like wildfire and I had offers on all my furniture. Our lease was up on May 1st and I had to move anyway.

We couldn't afford the big house anymore and this was my only option. When Ken finally called me, I told him about the decision I had made. I told him I wanted to join him and raise our children together in Miami as a family. To my surprise, he wasn't so enthusiastic about the idea. He said he needed me to stay in Montreal in case things didn't work out in Florida—at least then he would have his furniture and family to come back to. Great! I was a security blanket for him. I think not! I told him that if he didn't want me to move down there with him, I was getting a divorce. I then slammed the phone in his ear. I felt so lost. All alone with four children, running out of money which was limited to a welfare check. My life with the children was heading for disaster if I didn't do something, and fast. I knew we could make it if I went to Florida. With Ken's income we would be fine, as I would also find a part-time job somehow. I was convinced we could do it together.

I waited a couple of days and, like clockwork, Ken called me back. He told me to rent a smaller place until he had a better job. He said he would then call for us to come to Florida. I had no intention of doing this. I was selling our stuff. My decision was made. I knew I couldn't sell Ken's personal items, such as his hunting and fishing equipment. I also couldn't touch his girlie magazines. I guessed these items would be stored at his parents' house. Who knew? But I had to start. Ken told me to sell everything at 50% off.

The day of the sale came in late April 1973. It was a huge garage sale. Around fifty people showed up and bought all kinds of our household items. Wendy was only two months old at the time, Wayne was a year-and-a-half, Shawn seven-and-a-half, and Mark was ten. Mark didn't like the fact that I was selling his wooden desk. I told him we needed the money for airfare and that we would try our best to replace it. It hurt me to sell the children's items and furniture. After all, what was I facing by leaving Canada and moving to Florida? Was I making the right decision for the family? I was living on hope and hope alone. Right in the middle of the busy sale, I noticed Wayne's cough was worsening. He had been sick for a while but his cough was sounding horrible. A neighbour and friend who was present, Brenda, advised me that Wayne should be taken to the hospital and that she would look after the kids and the sale. She was a registered nurse and felt Wayne needed to be seen right away. She put me in a taxi cab and off to the Montreal Children's Hospital I went. We wait about three hours to be seen. The doctor prescribed some meds for his cough and then we came back home. It was always better to be safe than sorry. To my surprise, when I arrived home, all the kids were asleep and just about everything in the house had been sold! Brenda was a lifesaver. I couldn't stop thanking her for her help. She made a pot of fresh coffee and told me to relax. She told me that Ken was lucky to have such a courageous wife to just pack up and leave and start fresh in another country. Little did she know all the trouble Ken was in, and I wasn't about to tell her either.

The next day Ken's mother called me. She said someone wanted to talk to me on the phone. Everything was always in code. She and Ken's dad believed the police had tapped their phone so they would never say Ken's name. I listened and Ken said that he had not found a house for us yet. I almost fell off my chair! Here I was, having sold everything we owned, and my husband didn't have a house for us yet? I even had transfer papers from the children's schools. I panicked and started to cry. Ken tried to reassure me it was just going to take some time and to pack the rest of the items and get ready to go to Plattsburgh.

I had a friend put my dishes and personal items at my mother's place. The next morning, Ken's friend Alfie came to pick us up to drive us to Plattsburgh. When he came inside, the first thing he did was yank the phone wires from the wall. I asked him why he was doing this and he just muttered that Ken had asked him to. As I was leaving our home, an abundance of sadness came over me. I loved that house. I loved the neighbours and the fact that the schools were close for the boys. I must have been crazy to do what I was about to do. Let me tell you, love does make people to some crazy things!

In no time, we were in Plattsburgh. Ken met us there outside of the motel. He was standing in front, already waiting. Alfie helped take our things to the motel room. It was small: one bedroom for all of us and a small kitchen. I wasn't impressed at all by the motel room, but Ken said it wouldn't be for long. After Alfie finished helping us, he left for Montreal. The minute he left, Ken asked me for $500 for the first month's rent in Plattsburgh. Staying in motels back in the day, they wanted the money up front in advance. I thought he had some nerve to ask this, but I stayed calm and gave it to him. I gave it to him with hope in my heart that he would call me in a few weeks from Florida, telling me he had found a house for us to rent and that we would finally be reunited as a family.

The very next day, he left with Mark and Shawn for Florida. He said once he found us a house to rent, he would let us know and we would all be reunited again. His Aunt Ethel came to the motel and she stayed with us. The children loved her and that made it a little bit easier for everyone at the time.

Wendy had a bad case of diarrhea. I didn't know where it came from, whether it was the food or the water, but it sure was bad. I called her doctor in Montreal and he told me only to give her bottled water. The days passed and it rained every day. I was starting to get depressed. I had to walk through a mud path daily just to go to the laundromat. With young children, I had no choice but to do laundry daily. Days turned into weeks, and still Ken hadn't found us a house. I barely heard from him. He did get his job back selling wigs, but what I needed to hear was that he had found a house and that our future was now secure. He told me that when he was at work, his neighbour Suzie was the one looking after Mark and Shawn. Then, a couple of days before the month was up, he called me and told me he had found a house for us to rent. Finally! I couldn't have been happier. I ran from the motel office to tell Ethel. Our room didn't have a phone in it so every time I had to make a call, I had to go to the motel's office. Ethel called Alfie to come and get us. Alfie came the following day to drive us back to Montreal to say our farewells.

It was a nice little farewell party. My brother Joe planned all of it. It was at my mother's house and all of the family managed to attend. It was nice of them to wish me well. I hadn't seen them much since the children were born, and all the stress I had to deal with on a daily basis was so unsettling that it felt so good to be happy for once.

My brother Joe drove us to the airport the next morning. I really didn't like flying. It made me sick to my stomach. I had a lot of anxiety when I flew and had to take Gravol to settle my stomach. Wayne and Wendy were fine with the plane ride. There wasn't that much turbulence, so it went quite smoothly. I had time to think on the plane while the kids slept. How would Ken act once we arrived? What would the house look like? Would we be able to make things work? Would Ken apologize for all the stress he'd put his family through over the past couple of years? It was all too much for me to think about, so I took a nap.

When we landed in Miami, Ken and the two older boys were there to meet us at the airport. Ken had a nice yellow Mustang. The boys were very excited but my husband was acting cold and very strange. He seemed more like a taxi driver than a father.

We drove for some time and then finally arrived at the house. Ken barely said a word the whole time in the car. He drove up to our house and then said to me, "I hope you will appreciate all I've done for you." I almost died when I entered the house. It was like a horror film. The house was filthy. He unpacked our items and then went right out to the store to buy a highchair and playpen. We ate out at a restaurant and then returned to our so-called home. I put the two younger ones to bed and then told Mark and Shawn to put on their

PJs. Ken then told me that Mark and Shawn would not be sleeping there tonight, as he didn't have time to pack any of their clothes at the place he was staying. He said Frank's daughter, Bonnie, was in town and that she had another week to look after them. He also said he hadn't told his landlady that he was moving, as she was away, and he had to take care of the building for her until she came back. I couldn't believe what I was hearing.

I pleaded with my husband that I couldn't stay alone in the house with the two younger ones. I didn't know anyone, I didn't have any money and there wasn't even a telephone in the house! He then became very hostile. He started screaming at me, calling me every name in the book. He was throwing things around and said he never should have brought me to Florida. He then slammed the door and left with the two older boys.

I was petrified. Once I put Wayne and Wendy to bed, I started cleaning the house as much as I possibly could. The house was full of palmetto bugs. They were not like the bugs back in Montreal—they were enormous and they actually flew! Once I was done cleaning, I sat down and just cried. I though the next-door-neighbour Suzie was babysitting our children. Who the hell was Bonnie, and why was she babysitting our kids?

The next morning Ken dropped off Mark and Shawn and rushed off to work. I didn't even get a chance to ask him anything. The boys had a lot to say, though. Shawn told me that he saw his father patting Bonnie on the bum sometimes. He told both boys not to tell Bonnie about Wayne or Wendy, as this news would only make Bonnie cry.

That evening, I demanded that Ken bring home all of Mark and Shawn's clothing, as well as his own. He brought the boys' belongings, but as for his, this was not the case. He told me the landlady was still out of town. He said he still had to take care of the dwelling until she returned and, also, she didn't know about me. I asked him where the hell she thought the children came from. I then questioned him about Bonnie. Ken told me that Bonnie was Frank's daughter and that she was visiting. She was doing him a favour by taking care of the boys. I didn't have any more questions; I just wanted to go to sleep.

My days were mostly spent cooking and cleaning. I had to wash all our clothes and the baby diapers by hand each day. Twenty-four diapers to be exact. With no hot water, I had to boil water daily just to be able to do this and to give the children a bath. I was so sorry I had moved and disrupted our children's lives. I had to think of something. I actually needed a miracle.

My husband started to eat fewer suppers with us. It was bad enough he didn't even live with us; our children didn't understand why they were seeing less and less of their father. His excuses were the same: that the landlady was still away and he had to take care of the building until she returned.

Florida was known for their storms. With it being so hot during the day, night was the only time we could get some relief. One night, there was a terrible storm. The children were afraid of all the thunder and lightning so they decided to sleep with me. I had three boys all in my small single bed. It didn't bother me, as everyone was together. It was actually very nice and comforting. Then the doorbell suddenly rang at 1:30 a.m. I was too frightened to answer it. It just kept ringing and ringing. Who the hell could it be? I didn't know anyone in the area and who would be at my door at such a late hour? I had no telephone, so I couldn't even call the police. What was I supposed to do? I finally found enough courage to get up and sneak over to the front door. I looked out, and to my amazement, it was Ken screaming at me to open the door. Why didn't he use his key? I let him in and he kept screaming. He called me a bitch because I made him wait outside for so long. He said he didn't even know why he came by.

Ken put the children back to sleep and then I found out the real reason why he came home. Ken wanted sex. I was upset, so all we did was argue. He left and then came back again the following night. We had sex that night and he left again. I felt worthless. I felt like a prostitute. This was not happening to me. It all felt like a bad dream.

LADY NEXT DOOR

ONE MORNING AS I WAS HANGING MY DIAPERS outside, I heard a screechy old voice screaming at me from the backyard. I looked over to my right and saw the old lady next door almost hanging out her window, shaking her finger at me and calling me a filthy, sinful lady. I turned to her and said, "Are you speaking to me, Madam?" She then slammed the window shut and closed the blinds. What the hell was that about?

When Ken arrived after supper that night, I noticed him talking with her outside the house. When he came inside, I told him what she had said to me. He said she was the crazy landlady and that she was mad because I was hanging the diapers outside. He also told me not to worry because she was moving to California soon. This story made no sense at all but before I could question him again, he told me that Alfie and his wife were on their way down from Montreal. They were coming to rent the house next door for a while.

They were actually going to rent the house the landlady was in. At least now I would have someone to socialize with.

To heat the water in our house I had to depend on the sun. When it rained, I had to fill large pots of water on the stove for baths, etc. We didn't have a washing machine in our home. It was also quite difficult for me to take the babies out when I didn't own a stroller, either. So what I would do was sit on the front stoop with Wendy on my lap so she could get some sun.

At this time Ken was still telling me he couldn't move in because his landlady was *still* away. His other place was about six streets away from us. Wendy was four months old at the time. I couldn't take his lies anymore, so one day I decided to walk down to see the other house where he was living. Mark and Shawn were watching cartoons and I waited until Wendy had fallen asleep in her playpen. I got Wayne ready and told Mark and Shawn I was going for a short walk with Wayne and I would be right back. The sun was blazing hot that day. We only walked a few blocks and I had to return. The heat was so intense and Wayne was complaining about it the whole way. We made it to the street, but I turned back because of the heat. I wanted so badly to ring the doorbell. I wanted to see if Bonnie would answer. Ken happened to come home when we were on his street, and he yelled at me across the road.

"Where the hell did you come from, bitch?"

I gaped at my husband. "I just went for a short walk," I said.

"Well, do it again and I'll kill you. You're on my turf now so watch it!"

I yelled back, "Kenny, I travelled 3000 miles for us to be a family again and we don't even live or sleep together anymore. This isn't normal!" I was so embarrassed. I couldn't believe he had said those words to me and in front of Wayne, no less. I left the street as fast as I could possibly walk.

A few days later, Wendy came down with a very high fever. I didn't have a telephone in the house or a stroller to get her to a clinic; I didn't have Ken's number at work or his phone number for his other house; and I had no money to take a taxi to see a doctor. I gave Wendy a baby aspirin and waited for Ken to come by. Thankfully, he dropped in at lunchtime and once I told him about Wendy, we all got in the car and went to see the doctor.

The nurse took Wendy into another room and asked me to wait outside. I didn't like this. I then heard a blood-curdling scream come from the room where she was being examined. I ran into the room immediately and asked the doctor and the nurse why she was screaming like that. The doctor was extremely old. The examining room gave me the creeps, as well. I was told that they had to give her a needle due to the fact that her fever was so high. I was also given antibiotics for her throat. She had a very bad throat infection that would take some time to heal.

We arrived back home from the hospital and I put Wendy down to rest. The boys wanted to play outside so I ask Mark and Shawn to take Wayne outside. Upon seeing Wayne, the old landlady next door screamed and called him a bastard. I ran outside to give her a piece of my mind, but as soon as she spotted me she ran inside and shut the blinds. That's when I knew this woman had serious psychological issues.

That evening I couldn't sleep. I kept tossing and turning. I was hearing strange noises outside my bedroom window. It sounded as if someone was digging right outside my window. The windows were always kept shut because of the air conditioning, but I was positive that this was the sound. The next morning I went into the backyard to check, and I saw the landlady in her garden. I asked her if she heard any noises last night. She told me that her cat was outside very late. I checked the spot right under my window and I couldn't believe what I saw. The dirt was indeed turned over the size of a grave. Who in the hell had done this? I had to tell Ken.

I explained to my husband what I seen. He told me that I was as crazy as the old lady next door. Was I? Was there really a hole dug under my window or was I losing my mind?

I got so tired of the old lady next door calling me a sinner each and every time I hung out the diapers that I started hanging them inside the house. Even then I couldn't get away from her. She started peeking in my window and shaking her finger at me. The stress of how I was living was really getting to me. I just wanted to go back home to Canada.

It was a Sunday when Alfie arrived with his family. Ken said because of the fact that the old lady next door hadn't moved out yet, Alfie would have to live with us for now. I was ordered to adjust. Alfie and his wife came through the front door with their luggage and exclaimed, "Who in the hell is that crazy lady next door?" I told him it was our landlady. She had run up to Alfie's car with her large gardening shears and called him a bastard. Alfie said she moved away just in time because he was going to run her over.

I told Alfie all about her. I told him how I was treated like trash. Alfie told me he had paid Ken for one month's rent so I didn't have to worry for the time being. We split the rooms; each family had a bedroom to share. It was an extremely tight space to live in, but I was glad to have the company and didn't mind at all.

One evening, Ken took Alfie to see his other house. When Alfie returned, I couldn't wait to question him. I was told that Ken lived alone and I believed him. I told Alfie something was seriously wrong with our marriage. Besides the fact that Ken lived in another house, we didn't have sex at all anymore. Alfie told me that Ken felt very insecure and this was the reason he wanted to keep the other house. I really wanted to be understanding, but at the same time I had to think of my children. This wasn't healthy for them at all.

Three weeks passed. Alfie found a job and he and his wife rented a place on the other side of town. I really didn't want them to leave. It was bittersweet when they moved out and seeing the looks on the children's faces devastated me.

BACK TO MONTREAL

THAT VERY SAME WEEK, KEN CAME OVER AND TOLD me he had next to no money left and that I would have to return to Canada with the children. I told him if I was leaving then he was coming with us.

Ken said there was no way in hell he was leaving. He said that I was to go home with Wayne and Wendy, and he was keeping Mark and Shawn. That was when I lost it. I screamed at him, telling him he could do what he pleased, but I was going back to Canada with all four of my children. I started shaking because I knew Ken wouldn't like what I just said. I was petrified of him. But I truly loved my children and there was no way I was leaving without all of them. Ken screamed that he had no police warrants in the US, so he was staying in Florida. He called me a bitch and said the older boys were better off with him. I tried to ignore him. I walked to the closet and began to pack all our clothes. I could see that my doing this was making Ken angrier by the second.

Ken yelled, "Where do you think you're going with no money?" I told him I would go to the Canadian consulate if I had to. I told him I would stop a police car and ask them to drive me there if needed. I said, "I'll tell them all about you Ken . . . all about you!" I kept thinking about how day after day he left me stranded in the house with that lunatic woman next door. As I was carrying the suitcase into the parlour, Ken smashed my hand trying to knock the suitcase out of it. The pain was horrible! My heart was breaking at the same time at the thought of losing my two older boys. I went to get another suitcase to pack, and I could see my thumb swelling instantly. It was almost twice the size. I couldn't move my hand at all. Ken noticed this and ran to get me some ice. He called me every filthy name under the sun. I screamed at him to leave and then ran into the bedroom and balled my brains out like a little girl.

Once Ken left, I put ice on my hand and put the kids to bed. I took a painkiller to try and ease the pain. Believe you me, it was difficult to sleep that night.

The next morning Ken came to the house. He told me he was moving back to Canada with all of the children. I was so happy but didn't show any emotion. I was in the middle of scrubbing diapers with my broken thumb and was cursing him under my breath. He didn't once ask me how my thumb was. He told me to start packing after I finished with the diapers.

Back to Canada we went. The whole plane ride home Ken kept reminding me that he was only coming back for me and the kids. That he could be arrested any time after the plane landed and that I should be grateful that he was taking this chance for us. I just ignored him and daydreamed the whole flight. I was just so happy we were on our way back to Canada.

Ken's father was the one who picked us up at the airport. When we arrived at his house, he was so scared of Ken getting arrested that he brought in all the luggage. This disturbed me as he was such a frail old man. Ken should have been the one bringing in the luggage, but instead he ran into the house and made a beeline for his girlie magazines.

Here we were, living at Ken's parents' house, crammed together in a 3 1/2 and all Ken could think about was going back to Florida. I could hear him talking on the phone daily. I don't know who he called, but he always said it was the landlady. He said he was trying to keep the place he had there. He said there was no way he was going to jail because of me.

One night he received a call from Florida. Whatever the conversation was, it sure upset him because he ended up smashing the phone and screaming that his life was finished.

He went on, yelling how the landlady down there was evicting him and he had to remove all his belongings. I screamed back at him, "Doesn't this family mean anything to you, Ken? What the hell did you lose down there, anyway?" I told him we could rent a house here and our family should be the only thing he should be worried about right now. He continued to scream and started punching the wall with his fist. He was turning into a lunatic. His father told him that he would purchase the plane tickets in the morning so he could return to Florida. This calmed him down and then he went to watch TV.

The next day when Ken left for Florida, I told his parents how I had lived down there. I told his parents how I thought their son had a mistress. His mother immediately left the room and his father defended him all the way. He said Ken would never do anything to tear apart the family. He said I was just overreacting. Was I?

It was now Sept 1st, 1973, and I was broke. We were still living at Ken's parents' house. I applied for welfare again and enrolled Mark and Shawn in a nearby school. Life was hard. Ken's mother had just had a heart attack, and now they said the stress of the kids was too much for them to handle so we needed to find our own place.

I called my mother and explained the situation. She said I could come live with her and my father, but only with the two younger children. My sister Rosie said she would take Mark and Shawn for a while. I wanted all my children together but having this as my only option, I agreed.

When Ken heard the news about his mother, he came back from Florida. He wanted the two older boys to live with him until I got a place. I agreed. Rosie insisted that it wasn't a problem for them to live with her, but I didn't want to put her out. Ken came to get them and I stayed at my parents' with the two younger ones.

One night, Ken called me and he was crying. He explained that his mother couldn't take care of the children anymore and that he was at a motel with them. I couldn't have my children living like that, so I had to move fast. I asked my brother-in-law Alex to drive me around LaSalle to look for places. I finally came across one on First Avenue. It was a very small 4 1/2 in my budget. I knew I could make it a cozy home for the children, so I took it.

TWO LIVES

DAYS PASSED AND OUR HOME WAS STARTING TO feel quite cozy. Ken's mother called me and told me that Ken wanted me to come over because he had something to discuss with me. I went over and my husband bluntly came out and told me he had a girlfriend in Florida named Bonnie. He said he was going back to Florida to be with her and he didn't want me to make a scene in front of Mark and Shawn. I wasn't surprised at the news but it sure did hurt inside. We were married! What kind of a man has a girlfriend when he is married? He had absolutely no remorse, no guilt and no shame. I took Shawn and Mark and left the house. I didn't tell him that I had found a place. I didn't want him to be part of our lives anymore.

My family helped me furnish my new place on First Avenue. It took me about a month or so to get the courage to call Ken's mother to let her know where we were living, in case she ever wanted to come and visit her grandchildren.

I told her not to tell Ken where we lived because I didn't want him knowing any of my business and didn't want any more grief. It didn't do much good because two days later I found out she had told him, anyway.

One evening, Ken showed up at the door. He came to tell the boys that he was returning to Florida to make a new home for all of us. He said once he was settled he would send for all the children. Could Ken have finally been sorry for all he has done? I guessed time would tell.

We were now in December of 1973, and things were calming down. The children were adjusting well in our new house and even starting to make new friends. Ken started sending us letters from Florida. The letters annoyed me because they always said the same old thing. He always said how he missed us all and how the weather down there was perfect. Why in the hell would we care if the weather was perfect? His family was here in Montreal, starving, barely making ends meet, and all he did was brag about the great weather in Florida? His words sickened me. His letters annoyed me and his lies tore apart my soul.

On Christmas I received a call from Ken saying how he had lost weight and that all his hair was falling out. He begged me to go down to Florida with the kids. I don't know what I was thinking, but I agreed to go down for about a month or so, to see what happened and then decide what to do from there. Who knew, maybe I could get a little rest down there. I was so stressed. I had lost twenty pounds and wasn't eating properly because I was saving all the food for the children.

Off we went to Florida for the second time around. When we got off the plane, Ken was there to meet us at the airport. The minute I saw him I knew I had made a mistake because, as usual, he was stone-cold with me. He was affectionate with the boys but not with Wendy. He wasn't losing his hair by any means but he had lost some weight. I didn't know what he was up to this time, but I knew he wasn't sincere.

When we arrived at Ken's house, his friend Alfie and his wife Ruth were there with their children. I was asked to serve them dinner because they had to leave soon. How was I supposed to do this? I didn't even know where the food or the fridge were. The nerve of my husband asking me to make dinner for his friends the minute I walked into the house.

Alfie left after some time and I finally got a tour of the house. I asked him where his girlfriend Bonnie slept. He replied that she slept on the couch, as she was a lady of class. I ignored his remark because I didn't believe a word of it.

I got up early the next morning to unpack our things. Ken was already at work and I was stuck once again without a telephone or any money at all. I started to clean the bureau and spotted a picture of a blond woman taken in Paris. This upset me terribly but I searched further. His bottom drawer contained many papers. One paper in particular stood out to me. I couldn't believe what I was reading. I found a paper in my husband's drawer that stated he was divorcing a woman named Bonnie Jeanne Robinson. I read it over and over. My heart started beating so fast. The pain was horrible. I didn't know what to do. I couldn't confront him because I was too afraid, but at the same time, *I was married to a bigamist!*

A marriage of deceit was indeed what we had. How could I have not known about this? How long had he been married to her? Questions upon questions ran through my brain. I had no answers. As a matter of fact, I had nothing. I felt nothing. I was so shocked and saddened at the same time, it was horrible. I knew Ken would be back for lunch soon, so I had to put the items away and start making his lunch.

Ken walked through the door not too long after. Nothing was made for him to eat. The yelling and screaming started.

"What in the hell is the matter with you, Ann?"

I just stared at him. He asked me the same question again.

"What in the hell is the matter with *me?* What in the hell is the matter with *you*?" I said. "How could you lie in front of God?"

I got up, went to his top drawer, took the picture of the woman the boys had described as their baby sitter and ripped it up to pieces right in front of his face. Not a second later, his hands were around my throat. He was choking me. Somehow I broke loose and ran to the kitchen, but he chased right after me, calling me a bitch. He was yelling that that was the only picture he had left of Bonnie. He started beating me quite brutally. Again his hands were around my throat. This time I couldn't get away and I could barely breathe. Ken was screaming that I was going to make him lose this house and that he didn't want to go back to Canada to face his charges. He finally released the tight grip around my neck and told me the only reason he wasn't killing me was because I had to take care of the children. He said he divorced me in Reno and Bonnie had all the papers. He then went out the door and back to work.

My body was bruised; my heart and soul were crushed. I was terrified to go to the police. Something inside me died that day. I felt so empty. Tears kept filling up in my eyes as I continued my day. The boys sensed there was something wrong. What was I to do?

Ken came home from work that evening quite calm. He said he forgave me for snooping in his drawers. All he did that night was talk about Bonnie and her dad. I realized he was still in love with her and there was nothing I could do.

It was about a month before Ken finally bought Wendy a stroller. The minute I got the stroller, I went for a walk with Wayne and Wendy. Mark and Shawn were in school so it was easier for me to get around. I walked to a telephone booth and called the minister who had married Ken and Bonnie. I told him how upset I was and that I wanted to see him at our house. The Reverend told me that when he married Ken and Bonnie, he didn't even know Ken had any children until Mark and Shawn came down to visit. He was quite taken aback when I told him Ken and I never divorced and that we had four children. The Reverend then told me that Ken was currently at his house with Bonnie and her dad. He was trying to get her back. I pleaded with him to help me get back to Canada. I wanted out. I needed out. This was a horrifying nightmare. He told me he couldn't help me financially, but to be patient because Ken was currently in a state of mind that he could kill someone. He didn't want me to be Ken's target.

Days went by and all Ken did was talk about how much of a bitch Bonnie was. He was trying to convince himself that he still cared for me. Day in and day out he plotted his revenge on Bonnie's dad. He blamed him for everything that went wrong in their relationship. Money wasn't flowing so I had to take a job babysitting two extra children. Taking on six children was exhausting, but listening to my husband complain about his other wife was beyond excruciating.

Finally, one morning, my prayers were answered. Two immigration officers showed up at our door. They were looking for Ken's working papers and he didn't have them. They gave us six months to pack up and leave.

One night while we were sound asleep, we were awakened by the sound of gunshots outside. I immediately ran to the children's rooms to make sure they were all right. Ken ran to the den and pulled out his shotgun and went to the front door. He ran outside and I followed him. The trunk of his car was full of bullet holes as was the wall beside our front door. The stillness in the air terrified me. Who was after my husband, and why? What if they harmed our children? I ran back into the house, ready to call the police.

Ken insisted not to call the police. He was convinced it was Bonnie's dad who arranged it. He said Frank hired someone to kill him. I asked him why Frank would do such a thing and he told me to mind my own business. I guess his wife wasn't worthy of an answer.

I had been back in Florida for nine months now, and I was miserable as hell. We never went to the beach once.

The poor kids were only brought to the park twice and once to the zoo. I couldn't wait until the day we went home.

About a week later, Ken declared it was time for us to leave. Ken had rented a Grand Prix in Florida and this is the car we drove home in. I had never been happier in my life to return to Montreal. I knew it would be the last time I would ever go back to Miami.

Three days on the road with irritable kids and a husband who was ready to explode was a nightmare.

We finally made it. It was August 1974, late afternoon. I was so tired. Wendy had been on my lap the entire drive home. I got out of the car, struggled with all the luggage and brought it upstairs. Ken sat in the car combing his hair and straightening out his pants. He finally came upstairs and starting pulling down all the blinds. I told him we had to be able to see outside and pulled them back up. He threatened me and called me a stupid bitch and said I would be to blame if he was arrested. I ignored him as usual and continued unpacking.

In the days that followed, Ken kept checking the windows daily, washing his hands excessively and combing his hair every twenty minutes or so. It was driving me crazy. He caused me to have ulcers from being so nervous all the time. He was constantly picking on us, blaming everyone in the house for all his problems.

We had absolutely no income so I had no choice but to apply for welfare once again. Ken's parents also helped and I was lucky enough to get some aid from the local church for food. I wouldn't want my husband to work and take care of the household. I guess that would be asking for too much. How could he work, anyway, when he had a warrant out for his arrest? What a great father figure I had for my children. I was so down in the dumps for letting myself go back to a situation that I knew wouldn't work.

THE ARREST

I DIDN'T REALIZE AT THE TIME HOW SICK KEN REALLY was. His psychological problems were way more than we could handle. Every time the doorbell rang, my husband would run and crawl into a corner hiding. He was afraid that whoever came by would tell the police he was there. He even purchased another .38 revolver while we were in Florida, stating that he might one day need to protect himself. I begged him to get rid of the gun. He told me it was out of the question and to stop bothering him about it.

I went to the doctor as I started losing more and more weight. I was thin as a rail, barely 110 pounds. The doctor prescribed me some Valium. I was advised to take only one daily. At first they helped, but as time went on I increased the dosage to three or four a day. My husband had us all living like prisoners. No one was allowed in our house and every move we made, he had a negative comment about it.

Ken used to scream so often that I remember going out on my nightly walks hoping to die.

The winter of 1974 arrived without warning. One morning after Mark and Shawn left for school, the doorbell rang. It was the police. They had two patrol cars downstairs blocking our driveway entrance where Ken's Grand Prix was parked. They kept ringing the doorbell and Ken instructed me not to open the door. He told me to keep Wayne and Wendy quiet. They finally stopped ringing the bell. Mark and Shawn came home for lunch. The minute they left, the doorbell started to ring again. Ken made a mad dash out the back door. He jumped the fence and ran through the deep snow. I answered the door now that Ken had left. I played dumb. I told the officers that Ken wasn't in the house and hadn't been. I told them I didn't know where he was. They searched the house and also opened the back door. They then saw the recent footprints in the snow and knew I was lying. The police officer told me he knew the footprints were Ken's because he said when he checked earlier that morning they were not there. I had nothing to say; I stayed silent as they rummaged through my home. They asked who the Grand Prix belonged to and I told them it was Ken's. One of the detectives came back in the house with a set of papers from Ken's glove compartment. They were the divorce papers from Bonnie. They called a towing service to come and get his car. The officer told me that if Ken wanted his car back, all he needed to do was to go to the police station to retrieve it. Little did he know that he was now facing new charges. Bonnie's father, Frank, was now trying to hit him with a bigamy charge.

Ken went to hide out at his aunt's house. Ethel called me a couple of times telling me that he was driving her nuts. "Welcome to the club," I would tell her. He was calling the house a lot, too. He wanted to take the boys to Plattsburgh. I refused, of course, because they had school. The kids didn't care because going to Plattsburgh meant getting out of school, shopping and toys. They didn't like to hear no for an answer and started giving me trouble. I started hanging up on Ken when he called because I couldn't take his constant screaming and threats. That didn't go over well because two days later he had our phone cut.

My brother Joe showed up at my door and ask what happened to my telephone. I burst out crying and told him what Ken did and how I was trying to get a divorce. I normally held all my emotions in but I just couldn't take it anymore. I told him about the ulcers and the Valium I was getting addicted to. He called Bell Canada right away from a payphone and had them reconnect me.

My brother then told me to let him know if Ken ever bothered me again. That afternoon, my telephone rang and it was the police. They had my two boys, Mark and Shawn, at the police station. Ken had been arrested. One of the police officers had spotted Ken at a nearby bank and called in a squad car to arrest Ken. I went down to the police station and picked up the boys. They were crying and very worried about their dad. My heart broke for them, but at the same time I was so upset that Ken would go outside with them knowing he was wanted by police. They didn't give me a lot of information about the exact charges against him. I didn't ask too many questions because all I wanted to do was get the boys home.

That evening, my brother came over. I told him Ken had gotten arrested. He immediately left our house and went down to the station. When he returned, he told me all the charges that Ken was facing. The red car that we drove home from Florida in had been reported stolen, he had his bigamy charge, his fraud charge and a whole bunch of other accusations that blew my mind! My brother was taken aback when I told him I was petrified of Ken. I guess I'd hidden that part of our relationship very well.

Days passed and I was getting anxious. Mark and Shawn kept asking when their father was coming home and I had no answer for them. I did receive a call from Ken's lawyer and he asked me to come down to the courthouse. I went down when the older boys were in school. The lawyer brought me into a small room. He sat me down and read me the charges that Ken was facing. He then asked me to lie for my husband so he could get bail. He advised me to tell the judge that Ken was looking after me and the children all the times he missed court. I stood up and told the lawyer that there was no way in hell I would lie for Ken when the actual truth was that he deserted me and the children in my last month of pregnancy with Wendy. He went to Florida and married someone else and he had the audacity to ask me to lie for him? The lawyer stood up with no sympathy or empathy at all and asked me to leave.

It was a waste of my time. Ken made bail anyway because his parents signed for him. The same day he made bail was the same day he started harassing me again. He started with crank calls and threatening to kidnap the children.

I finally made a long-awaited decision. I went to a lawyer and started divorce proceedings. The lawyer advised me to first file for a legal separation and then, if in six months I still wanted to proceed, I could continue with the divorce. The judge demanded that Ken be placed in a mental institution for a month because of all the threats towards me.

It was so peaceful when he wasn't around. It didn't last very long, though. The day after Ken was released from the Pinel Institute, he started with his bullshit again. One evening around 3 a.m., I had the fire department show up at my house with five trucks and a firefighter with an axe, ready to chop down my front door. I had to tell him it was a false alarm. How embarrassing! Another night Ken came himself and put his finger on the doorbell, producing a constant ring. I didn't answer the door and this really upset him, so he punched the glass door, putting his fist right through it, then left.

THE CABIN

DURING HIS STAY AT THE PINEL INSTITUTE, KEN lied to the doctors. His story was that I was the trouble-maker. Ken's IQ was very high and I was convinced that they believed whatever story he presented to them because they gave him an early release.

One day I was waiting for Mark and Shawn to come home from school. They usually arrived at 4 p.m. It was now 4:20 p.m. and I was starting to get worried. I called the school and they said the boys had left with all the other students and maybe they'd stopped off at a friend's house. The phone rang and it was Ken. He said that he wanted to speak to Mark and Shawn because he just got out of the institute and wanted to see them. I told him they hadn't come home from school yet. He then started yelling at me, telling me that I should know where they are and if they were lost he was going to kill me. I hung up on him. He kept calling and calling. I had a feeling Ken had the boys and was trying to make me feel like a bad mother. I called the police for help.

Around 8 p.m. the police finally showed up. They wanted pictures and a lot of information on Mark and Shawn. I was then told that Ken had reported the boys as missing, as well. When I gave the police officers their pictures, I died inside. Please, let my boys be safe!

I didn't sleep at all that night. I survived on coffee, coffee and more coffee. By the time morning arrived, I was so dizzy that I could hardly walk straight. I had to pull myself together because I had Wayne and Wendy to take care of. I called up the lieutenant who knew Ken. He told me he was almost certain Ken had the kids and wasn't telling anyone. He thought that otherwise Ken would have been searching and begging the police to search for the children, as well.

Boy, was he right! The next morning Ken called me and told me he had Mark and Shawn and was on his way to get the other two. I was so mad I hung up the phone. He kept calling and calling.

I jumped at every little noise I heard. I even pictured in my mind Ken shooting off the doorknob and coming in to grab Wayne and Wendy. I called my brother Joe. I asked him to help me. He came over and told me to get the kids dressed. My brother told me I needed to rest. He said that if I didn't, I was going to collapse. We brought the kids over to Ken's mother's house. Ken was there with Mark and Shawn. Joe also called the police officer to make him aware that Ken did indeed have the boys, and that we were also giving him Wayne and Wendy. Ken didn't want to take all four, but Joe insisted.

Joe and I then left Ken's mother's house and he insisted that I go to the country with him and Gail, his wife. He told me I needed to rest for a few days and once I got my strength back, I could go back home and get the children because Ken didn't want them.

The rest felt wonderful. Joe cooked all the meals and the country air was so fresh. There were daily walks in the woods and nightly fires on the wood stove. I felt at peace, the way one should feel.

I arrived back home a couple of days later. Within a few hours, Ken's mother was at my door with all four children, begging me to take them back. The children were so happy to see me and I felt alive again.

The court proceedings for my divorce started about a month later. So much time was wasted. Ken kept postponing every time we had to show up. The harassment didn't stop either. He sent sick telegrams, threatened me verbally and followed me. There were never any witnesses, though. I was so paranoid that I started taking more Valium and cried myself to sleep nightly.

There was never enough to eat. Once a month, I had to call the church for food. We got by on a lot of potatoes and rice. A lot of soup and sandwiches, too. I was lucky that I had my family to help out a little. We always seemed to manage and I was very grateful for any help I received.

Ken's mood suddenly started changing. He started sending me flowers instead of threats. I didn't want the flowers, but it was a relief for the children and me. I didn't need flowers. What I needed was food for the family.

The court date for our divorce was quickly approaching. Ken was coming around the house a lot more. The older boys were almost begging me to let their dad back in the house. They didn't want to see the evil in their dad. All they wanted was the fighting to stop. I refused and they started to disobey me. They took off with their father a lot and didn't return for days on end. When they did come back, they would show me the gifts he would buy them. I tried explaining that a father should be buying them food and not gifts. They didn't want to hear it. Mark and Shawn were brainwashed so badly that they started being very rude and disobedient. I had a small miniature plastic hockey stick that I spanked them with a couple of times.

COURTHOUSE BETRAYAL

KEN FOUND OUT THAT I HAD SPANKED THE CHIL-
dren on occasion and served me with papers in court. I
knew I was a good and devoted mother. People would often
tell me I was too soft. I always did my best, so I knew that
anything he said in court wouldn't stand a chance. I would
need witnesses, though. I had the school's truant officer
whose bones Ken threatened to break one time during a
heated argument, and my brother, Joe, who knew everything
that was going on.

One day, Ken disguised his voice and called our social
worker pretending to be his lawyer. He told the social worker
that at one point he had seen Mark and Shawn with black
eyes. He was insinuating that I did this to my boys. Ken said
the boys told him it was their mother who beat them. The
man was sick and full of deceit. He tried to put doubt in the
minds of all the people who knew me.

Our day in court had finally arrived. I would finally be free of this man and get my divorce. When I woke up to make the children breakfast, I noticed that Mark and Shawn were not in the house. I panicked and called Ken's mother right away to see if they were there. She told me they were. I was so upset because they had not said a word, just snuck out of the house to go meet their father. Social services sent me a babysitter for Wayne and Wendy. On my way to court I was wondering if Mark and Shawn were going to show up in court with their father. I wondered if they would lie to the judge. I brought the small plastic hockey stick as evidence.

As I was walking up the street towards the courthouse, I spotted Ken in a car with the two boys. Shawn yelled out, "Dad, look, there's Mom!" Crossing the street, my eyes filled with tears. I could hardly see but did hear the car racing at me. I came within a few inches of being hit. Mark yelled, "Daddy, Daddy, please don't hurt Mommy!" Ken then stopped the car quite abruptly. He got out of the car and told me the only reason he didn't run me over and kill me was because the boys didn't want him to. He called me a bitch and then got back in the car and drove off. I entered the courthouse and told my lawyer what had happened. We waited over an hour and then the judge finally dismissed the case because Ken never showed.

He started to butter me up once more. Love letters and flowers came by the dozen. When I would walk the children to school, he used to drive in his car alongside me and ask me for a date. Once, I found him in the backyard repairing the boys' bikes. His hands got dirty and then he came into the house to wash them. I guess he thought it was all right since I didn't say anything, so the following day he showed up with all his belongings to move in.

"What the hell are you doing?" I said. He replied that the boys needed him and that he would move out after the divorce. I gave in for the children's sake. The boys were thrilled to see him.

It was now 1976 and my divorce was granted. The lawyer knew Ken was in my house and warned me to get him out or he would never leave. I dropped all the charges against Ken. Ken warned me that if I ever went to court to testify against him, he would kill me. He was the same evil man as before he was arrested and I was a fool to ever let him back into my home.

Three years passed and Ken was worse than ever. Yelling and screaming daily was his thing. He liked to blame the family for all the troubles he had with his life. Ken became extremely fat and stopped bathing. He never tried to get a job. We were both on welfare and I wasn't allowed to work. He told me a woman's place was in the home, raising children. All he did was eat chocolate cakes and drink soft drinks.

I couldn't stand being poor. I landed up getting a job cleaning one of the children's teachers' houses. I was always paid at the end of the day. It was nice and I usually brought home steaks for the house. Ken wasn't happy that I was working; in fact, he started accusing me of having sex with someone else. My nerves were shot and all sexual desire I had for that man had gone straight out the window.

As for our household, all of our children had their own beds. Ken and I slept on a sofa bed. After a while he became so uncomfortable on it that he began waking up Mark and Shawn to sleep with me, and then he took the two single beds and put them together to sleep on them by himself.

BRIAN

IT WAS NOW 1979 AND A LOT CHANGED FOR ME. MY washing machine broke and I had to start taking my laundry to the laundromat down the street. One Saturday afternoon, while I was waiting for the cycle to dry, I spotted a very good-looking man entering the laundromat with a box of soap. He had a very nice physique. He started separating his wash and seemed to be having trouble sorting it all out. He didn't know what colours to wash with what. I chuckled when I saw this. The man noticed I was watching and smiled at me. He then asked me if I could help him sort his laundry. We talked a little. He told me his name was Brian. To my surprise, we were both divorced. I told him Ken was still living at my place and just wouldn't leave. That seemed to shock him and I wasn't quite sure if he believed me. I was thirty-nine, and for the first time in years I felt alive again. He was thirty-two. I didn't care. Age meant nothing to me. He asked me out for dinner. I immediately refused and told him Ken would kill me if he knew I was seeing someone. Again, I don't think he believed me. We said our goodbyes and I actually dreamt about him that evening. I was angry at myself for not accepting the dinner invitation.

I awoke the next morning and reminded Ken about the promise he made to leave the house after our divorce papers were final. He ran towards me, picked me up and threw me against the wall. He yelled that he would leave the house when he was good and ready, and not before calling me a stupid bitch. I thought every bone in my body had broken. I couldn't move. The children were so afraid. They just stared at me, waiting for me to get up. I waited until he stopped screaming and then I rose and went into my room and straight for the Valium again. He had thrown plates on the floor that broke. He ordered me to clean up the mess because it was my fault that he had to throw the items because I was being a bitch all over again.

I saw Brian again at the laundromat. We talked and he asked me out again. I told him I would let him know. I mentioned it to my friend Rose, and she was thrilled for me. Rose used to sell jewelry to make money. She had parties at people's homes and a lot of people would show up and sell their items. Rose told me to tell Ken that one night I would accompanying her to one of the parties. I thought it was a fantastic idea, but would it work? I was happy but petrified at the same time. The next time I saw Brian at the laundromat, I told him I would accept his invitation to dinner on one condition: that Rose came along as a cover. I don't think he believed me about Rose coming along, but he didn't say anything. He said he would like to go out on the following Saturday night and I agreed.

Saturday came and it was time for my date. I had gotten ready, put a little perfume on and dressed up a bit. Rose came over to pick me up. She had all her jewelry with her as a cover-up, in case Ken was watching. The plan was to go to Brian's house and then we would go out from there. We showed up at Brian's, and he was still shaving. He was taken aback when he saw Rose. It was at this point that I realized he didn't think I was serious when I told him about the way Ken was. Brian called one of his friends to come along and hopefully chat with Rose at dinner. His friend wasn't home so we decided to order pizza and stay in. We drank wine, ate and did a lot of laughing. Brian's television wasn't working so he went into the parlour and put on some music. I left Rose in the kitchen and followed him. We started to dance and when our eyes met, we kissed passionately. I was on cloud nine. We didn't stay too long in the parlour because Rose was there alone. We went back to the kitchen after about fifteen minutes and had a little more wine. It was getting late and I had to leave. I didn't want to leave. Brian made me feel so good and I hadn't had that feeling in such a long time. We kissed and he told me next time to bring the kids over.

I called Brian the next day from a phone booth while I was at the laundromat. He asked me to come by with the children. I explained to him that I couldn't and what Ken would do. He told me that he wanted to see me in person. I agreed to take a taxi to his place once I was finished with my laundry. When I arrived at his place, his eyes lit up. He was very happy to see me. I told him I couldn't stay for long. Brian told me that the fear I had of Ken was ridiculous and I had to do something about it. He said that wasn't a way to live. He was right. I then asked myself what the hell I was doing in this man's house anyway. I knew the answer: I liked him. He made me feel alive again. There was so much hate at home that if I could find the littlest piece of happiness, I wanted to take it.

We both agreed to telephone Ken and tell him. I picked up the phone and asked how the children were. He didn't answer me. He started shouting, asking me where the hell I was. I panicked and passed the phone to Brian. Brian started to talk to Ken. He introduced himself and then Ken cut him off and told him to call back because he had to make another telephone call. I told Brian not to call back because Ken was probably setting up a tape to record the call. Ken didn't want me to have anyone else in my life. I was terrified to go home so I stayed at Brian's that night.

In the morning, I phoned the police station for help. Lieutenant Mongeau knew Ken and all about his temper. He told me to see my lawyer. I went with the police to remove my children from our home. The police knew Ken owned guns so they didn't want to provoke him. Ken had said to the police that he was there because I had abandoned the children and spent the night at a man's house. I told them he was lying, but the police told me this was a civil matter I had to bring up with my lawyer.

Here I was, running from lawyers to the police. Nobody would take a stand and help me. I left and went back to Brian's. On the third day Rose and another girlfriend, Terry, came over to Brian's with a message from Ken. It was a marriage proposal. I told her to tell him to please just get out of my house and that my answer was no. It was all too much. I couldn't be happy. He wouldn't let me have a life. Brian asked if I wanted him and his friends to physically remove Ken from the house. I told him I wanted to do it legally.

I called Rose back and she started screaming. She told me that Ken went over to her house with his gun on his hip and demanded Brian's address. Rose was so scared that she gave it to him. She apologized over and over again on the phone for giving it to him. I hung up the phone and started trembling. I grabbed the telephone and hid under the table in Brian's kitchen. I called Lieutenant Mongeau. As I was dialing, the doorbell rang. I could hear Lieutenant Mongeau saying hello on the line, but I didn't want to answer because some of the windows were left open and I was too afraid Ken would hear me talking. I heard footsteps going upstairs to Brian's landlady's house. I then started talking to Lieutenant Mongeau, telling him all that happened. I begged him for help and gave him the address where I was. I hung up the phone and stayed hiding under the kitchen table. I was too scared to move. Too scared to blink and too scared to breathe.

There was a lot of yelling going on upstairs but I couldn't make out any of it. About forty-five minutes passed. The doorbell rang again. I heard Lieutenant Mongeau's voice. At last! I felt so relieved, I flew to the door. He came inside. He told me that Ken went to the landlady upstairs, posing as a detective. He told her he was working for in and outer worlds. She thought he was nuts and called the police for help. Apparently she had called just a few minutes after I did.

At this time, there was a warrant for Ken's arrest. I left Brian a note and left with the police. I started crying in the police station. I warned the police officers that Ken had ammunition in the house. Lieutenant Mongeau telephoned the house to tell Ken the police were on their way to remove him. He told the lieutenant to go fuck himself.

We were to all go back to the house to have Ken removed. This was not going to be easy. The station called in the SWAT team for the job. When we drove up to my house, what I saw was shocking. There were police lying on their stomachs on the ground in the backyard. There were police on my rooftop. There were police at either ends of the streets and in the laneway. I must have counted twelve police officers, including the SWAT team, all with bulletproof vests. I was terrified for my children. Would Ken try and shoot the police? Would the children get in the way of the gunfire? Why wouldn't he just give himself up and leave us alone?

Ken didn't answer the door. The police must have rung the doorbell at least five times. I heard orders from the police on their walkie-talkies to break down the front door. I prayed for my children. I prayed nothing would happen to them. Another voice came from the walkie-talkie. It was a police officer asking me if it would be all right if Ken's mother stayed with the children until I arrived back home. I told them yes, it was. I couldn't believe it! They finally got him out. He was out of the house!

I pulled up to the front door and was shocked. The door was pried open with a crowbar. How the hell was I going to fix that? I knew Ken would get bail again and I didn't even have a proper door to close. As far as the police were concerned, their job was done. I entered the house and my mother-in-law looked me in the face and said, "I hope your new boyfriend doesn't beat my grandchildren." I told her what Ken had done to me and she completely ignored me and left the house.

Wendy was the only one who welcomed me home. She had made me a bunch of drawings with hearts on them. She was the only one who made me feel welcomed. During that past week, my eldest son Mark had been vacationing with his girlfriend. He just looked at me and said, "Mom, I have one day left on my vacation and I don't want it spoiled."

LIKE FATHER, LIKE SON

I STARTED TO CLEAN UP THE MESS THE POLICE MADE when they raided the house, and I searched for Ken's guns and ammunition. I didn't find any of it. I wondered where he had put it. I tried making the house clean again and I knew I would have to explain to the children what happened.

The kids had a lot of friends and they would mostly go to their houses or congregate somewhere else. They rarely brought their friends home. I knew it was because of the life we had and I wished it could be different. Mark was always at his girlfriend Melody's house, Shawn was out with his friends playing tennis, and Wayne and Wendy were usually at the park. We had a park at the end of our street. We also had a dépanneur right across from us.

My children were not interested at all in meeting Brian. I asked Brian to be patient but he wasn't, so after a few heated arguments we stop dating. He started seeing my friend Rose. I was so hurt that it was all I could think about. My fear of

Ken eased as my heart was broken over Brian. I felt I had nothing left to live for.

A few days passed and I started having trouble breathing. The doctor ordered X-rays and they showed that I had pneumonia. I was given antibiotics and ordered to be on full bed rest for two weeks. I was so weak. I was so tired and depressed about losing Brian that all I did was take my meds and sleep in between caring for the children.

One morning, Rose called me. She asked me if I was upset that she had started dating Brian. She told me she was ten years older than he was and didn't know how long it was going to last. She wanted to have a little fun before she was too old. Tears fell from my cheeks as I wished her well and told her I was just hurt and not mad. She didn't seem to hear the pain in my voice and just hung up the phone after I let her know it was okay to date him. I guess her conscience was getting to her but obviously not enough, since she kept dating him after that.

Weeks passed and my pneumonia was getting better. I took my medication faithfully and rested like the doctor demanded. It was quiet in the house and the children were always doing their own thing. I went to the bathroom and noticed my underwear was full of blood. I was scared because it wasn't time for my period. The blood just kept coming so I went to the hospital. They told me that I either had a disorder or had just miscarried. I told Rose. She didn't tell Brian because she didn't want to lose him. I went home crying. I started to see less and less of Rose. I guess she was so busy dating Brian that she didn't have time for our friendship anymore. That was fine with me, anyway, because I didn't want to be reminded that he left me for her.

Mark and Shawn told Ken about me being in the hospital. One afternoon they actually let him in the house. He starting acting very concerned about my health. I burst into tears and told him about the pneumonia and the hemorrhaging. What hurt more than anything was my broken heart. It felt good to tell him all about it. He called Brian a drunken bum. He then asked if Brian had a larger penis than he did. I told him to get the hell out of the house.

When I was allowed off bed rest, Ken started to follow me. On two occasions, he tried to hit me with the car because I didn't want to speak with him. Ken didn't love me anymore, but at the same time, he didn't want me to have a happy life either. He blamed me for everything that had gone wrong in his life.

There was a policeman named John who took a liking to me. I never accepted his invitation for a date because of all the drama that was going on with Ken. One night, he called me and I agreed to go for coffee with him. Mark was now sixteen, so he babysat for me. I went to meet John. We drove in his car for a while and talked, then we stopped off at Dunkin' Donuts for coffee and doughnuts. We talked some more about our families. After a couple of hours, John drove me back home. I watched him drive away and then opened my front door. To my surprise, Ken was sitting on the staircase waiting for me. The boys must have let him in. His eyes were full of hate. He came at me with the pointed part of an umbrella. He started jamming it in my face, screaming that I was a whore for leaving my children at home alone while I went out with other men. Shawn begged him not to hurt me. He finally moved the umbrella out of my face, went and got his gun and wallet, and left.

Divorced, and still not free from Ken, how much more could I take? All the children were living at home except for Wayne. Wayne stayed at Ken's mother's most of the time. He told me he wanted to be with his father. Even if I would say no, Wayne would leave the house anyway. Wayne didn't go to school when he was over there. Ken didn't seem to mind, nor was he concerned that he missed school.

I went back to cleaning the teacher's house for extra money. Wayne and Wendy used to eat lunch at Rose's house on their lunch hour. Eventually, Ken found out that I was letting them do this and he threatened Rose. I told Rose I couldn't stop working because I had to feed the children.

Wendy kept going to Rose's for lunch, but Wayne stayed with his father.

Wayne was nine years old at the time. He started putting filthy notes in Rose's mailbox from Ken. It broke my heart that my son was learning this type of behaviour from his father. Wayne and I started to grow apart. He always took his father's side in an argument. Ken had Wayne brainwashed pretty good, and there was nothing I could have done about it. He was getting very rude and hard to handle. One day I smacked Wayne on the leg for talking back to me. As I did this, the telephone rang at the same time. It was Ken. Ken asked why Wayne was crying and I told him I had to discipline him because he was out of control and rude. I told Ken he should not involve our children in our arguments. Wayne then yelled out that I had broken his leg. Ken hung up the phone and came right to the house.

Wayne ran downstairs to let his dad in the house. Ken ran towards me, yelling that he was going to kill me. I was petrified. I couldn't move. He told Wayne to wait downstairs. Ken started pounding on my head with two closed fists. He wouldn't stop. I thought I was going to die. I fell to the floor from the impact of his blows. He kept yelling that he was going to finally knock some sense into me. Dragging me by the neck to the back balcony, Ken started pulling me towards the railing. I knew if he threw me over I would die. We lived on the second floor. I started screaming for help. Holding on for dear life to the railing, I spotted a neighbour. Ken then dragged me back into the house and ran downstairs and left. I lay there in agony. I couldn't move. Mark and Shawn weren't home, Wayne had already left downstairs and I didn't know where Wendy was. I lay all alone on my kitchen floor with multiple bruises and a possible concussion. Finally, I managed to crawl downstairs to the landlady's house on my knees and cried for help. She let me in and there stood Wendy. Wendy had run downstairs once she heard arguing. The police were called. After a couple of minutes, I called Mark at his girlfriend's house to come home and help me.

Mark helped me upstairs very slowly. My legs were like jelly. Every part of my body hurt. Soon after, the police arrived. They questioned me and I had to fill out a detailed report of what happened. They were extremely concerned about my head injuries and wanted me to get checked at the hospital. They advised me that Ken would be charged with assault and battery. Charged? What did this mean? I would have to go to court and testify against my own husband? I didn't know how much more of this misery I could take. Shawn came home a little while later, after informing me that Wayne was on the way to Plattsburgh with his dad.

I was tired of living. I didn't enjoy anything anymore. I was being abused mentally and physically, and I didn't see any light at the end of the tunnel. I fell to my knees asking God to guide me. I asked him for strength to find a way to get our family through these troubled times.

A month passed before Ken finally came back with Wayne. The school kept calling for Wayne and I had to keep making excuses each time as to why he wasn't in school. Either he was sick or had doctor's appointments. Those were the basic excuses. The day after Ken came back with Wayne, he was arrested for what he had done to me. Wayne completely blamed me and was so angry that's he ripped out the screen on the back door. He refused to go to school and instead took off and stayed at Ken's mother's house with his dad. Ken once again got bail.

HIT AND RUN

SHAWN WOULD VISIT HIS FATHER FROM TIME TO time. One night when Ken was bringing him back home, I heard the screeching of car tires outside the house. I immediately ran to the front door and at the same time the doorbell started ringing non-stop. It was Shawn. I opened the door right away and he started screaming that Ken was trying to run over Brian with his father's car. I told Shawn to get in the house and I picked up the phone to call the police. Mark slammed the phone down and told me that I wasn't calling the police on his dad. Two minutes later, there were three police cars outside the house. A neighbour must have called with all the noise.

Shawn explained to me that when he was on his way home, Ken saw Brian down the street walking towards the car. Brian was the one who asked Ken to get out of the car. When Ken refused, he then kicked the car. Ken reached for his gun in the dash, but Shawn's plea stopped him. He then kept trying to run Brian over and Brian kept jumping out of the way. My neighbour, Noella, was working in her basement and looked out the window to see what was going on. Ken spotted Noella and knew she would be a witness, so he took off down the street. It was another one of Ken's moments where he completely lost his temper.

A couple of hours later I had a visit from the police. Noella and Brian were also spoken to and they accompanied me to the police station. A charge of attempted murder was now put on Ken. To our surprise, Ken was already at the station filing a charge against Brian for kicking his car. He then left quickly and went to get Wayne and once again headed off to Plattsburgh.

I couldn't believe Ken would involve his nine-year-old son in all of this. Wayne was stuck in the middle and would do anything his father asked. I felt so hopeless inside. I didn't have Brian's love, I had a crazy ex-husband and children who were learning horrible things from the way their father was acting.

It was now September and a new opportunity to start fresh in school. Wayne and his two older brothers did not get along. It hurt Wayne when Mark and Shawn criticized their dad. Ken was a hero in Wayne's eyes. The fighting between the four children became unbearable. I was constantly playing referee and it didn't help that the house was so small.

In December 1980, Ken started romancing me again. He started sending me flowers and actually sending me money, as well. He told me he didn't want to live without the family being together.

BABY #5

On Mark's 17th birthday, we received an invitation to have supper at his grandmother's house. There were still bitter feelings in my heart towards Ken and his parents, but I decided to go for Mark's sake. Ken was very pale and quiet. It was a nice little dinner. They ordered chicken from St. Hubert. The kids always loved takeout. This was a treat since we barely had enough to eat on a daily basis, and ordering out was very rare. After dinner Ken asked me to go in his mother's room. When I entered the room, Ken had a ring and proposed marriage. I couldn't believe what I was hearing or seeing. Mark overheard as he was passing by to go to the bathroom. He yelled out, "Mom, please say yes and everything will be all right again!" My mind was running crazy. Maybe Ken had changed? Maybe he wouldn't hit me anymore? I knew he did love me even though it was in his own way. I pondered the proposal for a couple of minutes and said yes. The children were very happy. We could start over. We could finally be a normal family.

Ken and I went to a motel that night. Ken's parents babysat the children. It was magical. Ken was always so good in bed. He always pleased me and made me feel ecstatic. We didn't have sex often but when we did I never had a complaint. As we lay there in bed relaxing, Ken leaned over and pulled out some pills. He said he only had two and wanted us both to take one. They were suicide pills. "Let's die happy, Ann," he said. I told him he was crazy and that we had to make a good life for ourselves and the children. Was he bluffing? Nothing more was said, and we both ended up falling asleep in front of the TV.

On January 10th, 1981, we were remarried in a protestant church. It was a quick wedding since Ken was still hiding from the police. After the wedding, Ken stayed at his mother's house and I returned home with the four children. The police got word that I had remarried Ken, so they paid quite a few visits to the house looking for him. Ken was always travelling back and forth to Plattsburgh, as he didn't want to be arrested, so they never really knew where he was. I denied that I had remarried him and always told them I didn't know where he was.

I started missing my period on and off. Since I was forty, I thought I was probably starting early menopause. After not having my period for over two months, I decided to go and see the doctor. He immediately did a pregnancy test and I was told I was having a fifth baby and it was due September 20th. A fifth baby? This couldn't be true. How in the world was I going to raise another child under these conditions? I was happy and confused at the same time. I called Ken at his mother's house and told him the news. He immediately told me to go and get an abortion. I yelled at him that I was not going to kill the baby and hung up the phone on him. With all the problems I was having, the baby was going to bring a lot of joy into my life. I had a lot of hope.

The check-ups started. I had phlebitis in my legs and had to wear special stockings during my pregnancy. I noticed a big difference being pregnant in my forties compared to when I was younger. At that time, my washing machine was broken. I had to walk two blocks to the laundromat all the time. As my stomach grew, all the neighbours would stare at me. They didn't know I had remarried Ken, so I can imagine what they were thinking. Ken bothered me, frequently telling me how much of a fool I was to keep the baby. I didn't listen to him and continued to do the best I could, raising all of them by myself.

Time passed and it was getting a lot harder. I didn't have a baby shower, but I did get a few baby clothes from friends and family. September 21st, 1981, I gave birth to my fifth child, another boy. I decided to name him Keith.

SEPARATE WAYS

MARK WAS ALMOST EIGHTEEN, SHAWN WAS sixteen, Wayne was ten and Wendy was now nine years old. I considered myself blessed. My parental urges were fulfilled but I still felt very lonely. I longed for a man's love.

Ken was at his parents' house at the time of Keith's birth. He was still hiding from the police. He called the hospital to see how I was doing but never came by. I had to borrow money from a friend to take a taxi home with Keith.

It wasn't until a couple of months later that Ken decided he wanted to see Keith. He came over when Keith was awake. He just stared and stared at him. He didn't say too much, just held his little hand and smiled. As for me, Ken was still ice-cold. He had no love in his heart at all. He did say he wanted to come back home and try and make it work. I don't know why I agreed because, once again, I was hiding him from the police. I was just a maid to him. I would cook and clean and do laundry. Ken would never lift a finger. He would watch TV all day or read his girlie magazines. He was getting more paranoid as the days passed. He only whispered when he spoke, as he was afraid the neighbours would hear his voice and call the police. It was quite disturbing. My husband would walk around the house in his underwear with his gun attached in a holster on his hip. I would be taking care of the children and he would be combing he hair in the mirror for hours. It was crazy. We didn't even have sex anymore because I was always reminded of what I had done with Brian.

One afternoon I received a phone call from the police. They had arrested Shawn. His high school had been broken into and someone told the police Shawn was one of the boys involved in the robbery. Twenty minutes later, they showed up at the door. Ken ran and hid in the corner of the living room. He was thinner then, so he fit perfectly and wasn't able to be seen. The police searched the house to see what they could find from the robbery at the school. They went into the living room where Ken was hiding. The detective sat on the couch. He then turned to his right and spotted Ken coming out of the corner.

"Remember me, man?" Ken said.

The detective's face turned white. "Mr. Robinson, is that you?" he said. The detective told Ken he had lost a lot of weight. Ken didn't put up a fight. He got dressed and went downstairs to the police car.

Ken sat in a holding cell for a couple months. A couple of times I went down there to get his dirty clothes and wash them for him. I had no choice but to bring Keith and Ken didn't like the idea of that. I told him I didn't have a choice and if he wanted clean clothes then Keith was coming along.

When Ken finally went to court, the charges against him were all dropped. Noella, my friend and neighbour next door, dropped the charges as she knew it was what I wanted and that I was trying to start a new life with Ken. Brian never showed up, either; I'm not certain of Brian's reason, but it didn't matter. Ken was now home. Would he change for the better?

I guess I was hoping for a miracle. Ken became very cruel with everyone in the household. We were still on welfare and as the children grew older, it was getting harder and harder to support them.

I started buying old dolls and knitting beautiful outfits for them and selling them for a nice profit. I had to find a way to make extra money. Ken wasn't pleased and complained that all I cared about was my dolls. He was jealous of everything and anything that brought me joy. Ken started asking Mark to help out around the house, moneywise. He said he was old enough to do this. Mark resented this and ended up moving in with his girlfriend, Melody, and her parents. I was relieved because I was worried things would get violent between the two of them otherwise.

Shawn started to lose all interest in school and dropped out his senior year. I didn't know at first but found out he'd started smoking pot and drinking on a regular basis. Wayne was causing all kinds of problems with the teachers in school. He was skipping school most of the time but when he was there, he was always acting out. Wendy was quiet, into her sports and always at her girlfriend's house. At this point, she didn't give me much trouble. It was getting heated in the house because Ken was losing control over the boys. He would fake heart attacks just to get sympathy from the children, He would fall on the bed and say, "Wayne! Wayne, help me!" Wayne pitied him and didn't see through him. Ken used to send him to the corner store daily. If Wayne didn't want to go or was being defiant Ken, would smash his head in the wall over and over again. One day, Wayne had enough. Ken demanded that he go to the store and get his cakes and soda. Wayne told him to go to the store himself as he could use the exercise. Ken went for his throat. He took out his gun and pointed it at his head. Wayne then yelled, "Go ahead, Daddy, kill me. There's no point in living with you anyway!" Ken was stunned by this response and told Wayne he was crazy and walked away. My heart broke. My poor son was being abused by his father and I was so afraid and didn't see a way out to save my children.

The abuse was starting to be a way of life. Every night, he would take out his guns. Ken had a rifle, a .38 and a .45 revolver. He would put them on the kitchen table and polish his bullets. His reasoning for this was that he didn't want the people he was going to shoot to get infected. That was it. My husband was clearly insane. What was I going to do? Keith was two, Wendy was ten, Wayne was eleven, Shawn was seventeen, and Mark, nineteen. Ken would tell everyone in the house that one day he wouldn't be able to control himself and that there would be blood all over the walls.

One night I went to see my friend and neighbour across the street, Noella. I told her how unhappy I was and about all the things Ken was doing. She questioned me a lot about what exactly was going on. She couldn't believe how I was living. I explained to her that I was petrified to leave Ken and that he had threatened to kill all of us if I did. Noella then told me that I was dead anyway, staying in that house day after day. She said it was more dangerous living like that on a daily basis than it was taking a chance and leaving him. She said she would help me.

I went home that night and thought a lot about what she had said. Noella was a very smart woman. She, too, had been abused in a previous relationship and knew what I was going through.

FREEDOM

A FEW MONTHS PASSED, AND ONE DAY WENDY RAN inside the house in a hurry. She told me if the doorbell rang not to answer it. She said it was just someone chasing her. I answered it, anyway, and Wendy and another girl were yelling at each other. Keith came over to see what was going on. I didn't want him hearing the girls cursing at each other, so I moved him away from the front door. Keith panicked for some reason and started screaming. Ken started yelling now from the living room to shut Keith up or he was going to strangle him. With the girls yelling and Ken yelling, Keith started crying even louder. Ken got up off the couch and headed towards Keith. I cuddled him in my arms to try and calm him down. Ken grabbed him from me and dropped him on the floor. Keith screamed even louder! He picked him up by his shirt and Keith's face was turning beet-red. I ran up to Ken and slapped him in the face. I screamed at him that Keith needed comfort because he was upset. I will never forget the look on Ken's face when I slapped him. Never! He dropped Keith on the floor and started to kick him in the ribs. He was calling him a piece of shit that he'd made. I ran to Keith and scooped him up in my arms. All of a sudden, I felt Ken's gun pointed at my head. Pressing it to the left side of my temple he said, "Now you're going to die, bitch! No one slaps me and gets away with it!" Wendy started screaming, "No, Daddy, NO!" and fled down the stairs and over to Noella's house. I spoke very softly, begging him to let me go. I told him I was going next door to Noella's to calm down and have a coffee. He cocked the gun and took Keith out of my arms. I was frozen with fear. He then put his gun back in the holster and told me it was his house, and if I wanted to go, Keith was *not* going with me. I fled out the house as fast as I could.

The door was already open. Noella was waiting for me. She let me in and made me coffee. She listened to me as I told her the horror story. It took me about two hours but I finally called the police. Shawn came over to Noella's a couple of hours later, trying to coax me to go back home. He said that his father would never kill me and that his dad was calm now. I told him I'd made up my mind and wasn't going back and that his father needed to leave. Shawn left Noella's with a very sad face. Wayne was the next one to come over. Wayne started to cry. He told Noella that his father had also pulled a gun on him several times, but if he testified it wouldn't be safe for him to walk the streets. He was terrified of his father. He said his dad would hunt him down and kill him one day. What were we to do? Who would help us?

The police came about forty-five minutes after I called them. I told them the story and they went over to the house. About an hour later, the police returned but not with Keith. They told us that Ken said we just had a little argument as families do and Wendy ran out of the house because of this. He said that I left the house to go and get Wendy at Noella's. What a liar! I had no proof and no witnesses to what had happened. My only witness was my two-year-old son who was in the house with his abusive father. I cried and cried.

I crossed the street with the policemen to get my baby before I left for the women's shelter. Keith was in Ken's arms when I entered the house. I called for him and stretched out my arms. Ken knew he would go to me so he moved away quickly with him. The police officer, not having any evidence of what happened, asked me to get a few things and leave. Since we were married, I had to present a case in court before I could get Ken removed from the house. And since I didn't have full custody on paper, if the kids wanted to stay with Ken there wasn't anything I could do until I saw a judge. I was so hurt. I just walked down the stairs and cried.

Wendy and I left in the police car to the woman's shelter. It was downtown on Rene Levesque, at the corner of Guy. It was in the basement of a large convent. The nuns were dressed in plain clothes and very pleasant. I couldn't sleep the first night. I was so worried about Wayne and Keith. I knew Shawn and Mark were old enough to take care of themselves, but Wayne was so brainwashed and terrified of his dad that I didn't know what would happen. Keith was only two. He couldn't even talk or tell anyone how he felt. It was a long night. Wendy kept waking up with nightmares, screaming that she saw Ken in the window with a gun. I knew they were just nightmares because the convent was secured by a very large fence and security guards placed outside for our protection.

Noella knew how worried I was about the children. She watched the house all day to make sure Ken didn't leave with the kids to Plattsburgh. Her husband, Peter, wasn't afraid of Ken and was willing to stop him if he spotted him leaving. I called the Ville-Marie Social Service Centre and told them my story. Noella also called them and tried to have them remove Wayne and Keith from the house, but the same story was told to us. We had to wait until the case went to court because I didn't have custody papers because we were married.

In the meantime, Noella and Peter sat on the front porch every day watching our house. They watched to see if Ken would leave the house with Wayne or Keith. Peter used to take his large knife and sharpen it on the front balcony, hoping Ken would be looking out the window. He wasn't afraid of Ken at all. He told me that Ken would order a lot of restaurant food and that the blinds were always down. Ken would peep out them several times daily.

It had been over a week and social services still had not brought the children to me. Noella called them again and told them if they didn't bring Wayne and Keith over to the shelter within an hour, she was going to call all the TV stations and tell them the story. She told them the children were in danger, and it made no sense that they were still in the house. Within an hour, Keith was brought to me. Wayne didn't come. He was too afraid of his father and told the police that Ken was not abusive and that he wanted to stay with his dad. I knew Wayne loved his dad, but it was the abuse I was worried about. How many more times was he going to hit him or smash his head in the wall when he didn't listen? Ten minutes later, I found out they had placed Wayne in a foster home for the time being since he didn't want to come with us to the shelter. I was heartbroken. I loved all my children and wanted them safe with me.

When Keith arrived I couldn't believe it. He was at least ten pounds lighter than when I had last seen him. Ken obviously hadn't been feeding him properly. I checked him for marks of abuse but didn't find any. I bathed him right away and cuddled him, as well. He was frightened of everyone. He didn't talk or want to play at first. The nuns tried to get him to. There were times I had to leave him with the nuns because of appointments with my lawyer and the court, and he would scream and scream as I was leaving. It was heartbreaking. There was a young teacher there who had a lot of patience with Keith. It took about a month but they became pretty good friends. The nuns kept asking me what the lawyer was doing for me. It was starting to look hopeless. My family was all split up and the court was taking so long to help me get Ken out the house.

THE SHELTER

I RECEIVED NEWS FROM NOELLA THAT KEN HAD started walking up and down the street with his shotgun like a soldier. The neighbours were terrified. He wouldn't say a word. He would just pace up and down the street with his shotgun on the side of his hip. All the social workers were getting threatened. It was all done in a manner where there was no proof. A morgue car was sent to social services with instructions to pick up dead bodies. Everyone was receiving threats. Noella would tell me she received a lot of threats from Ken but ignored them all.

There was also a lot of tension in the shelter. One night when the children were all in bed, all the women decided to have coffee and cookies in the kitchen. It was 11:30 p.m. The main doorbell kept ringing and ringing. One of the guards said it was a black man screaming at the door. There was a black woman in our group. She peeked through the hole. It wasn't her husband. The man had a shotgun with him. Somehow, he'd gotten past the guard who was on duty patrolling the grounds. The guard inside telephoned the police immediately. We heard the man outside screaming, "Where are you hiding my wife?" Florence, the black woman said, "Man, I am the only black woman in here! He might just think I'm his wife and kill me!" We all went to the corner where she was crouched and consoled her. The police came not long after and arrested him.

A couple of days later Keith came down with the flu. He had an extremely high fever and had to be taken to the hospital. That week all the children in the shelter were sick with the flu. Then Noella called me and told me that Wayne had run away from the foster home and was back at the house with his dad. I was mortified. Why would he want to go back to that monster? The police intervened and put him in a detention centre for his own protection. He didn't like that at all. Wayne actually found the phone number of the shelter and called me. He begged me to get him out. I told him he could have come with us from the outset but he wanted to be free and roam the streets all hours of the night. I tried to tell Wayne the shelter had rules. I told him I wanted him with me but that he would have to stay with us at the shelter for now. He got very angry and hung up the phone.

Meanwhile, Ken had fake papers made up claiming that he had divorced me in Florida and that he had full custody of Wayne, Wendy and Keith. He went to the court with these papers while we were in the shelter. When it was time for me to have my court date, the judge was so confused he delayed it for another month.

Off I went back to the shelter. Back to the unknown, where my children were so unhappy. My nerves were shot. We had been at the shelter for over three months now and I still had no idea when I could have my children back and get Ken out of the house and return home. Wendy was changing. She was being so defiant. Noella and Peter often came by the shelter to take us out for supper.

A couple more months passed and Ken repeatedly did not show up in court. After the fourth time, the judge finally got so fed up that he ordered Ken out of the house until the final divorce proceedings. He gave him three days to leave. At last I could go back to my house. What was I in for? I knew the battle between Ken and myself had just begun.

A NEW BEGINNING

It was now the summer of 1985. I felt so relieved going back home. A police car came to pick me up at the shelter. I was escorted back home by two detectives. Wendy and Keith were still at the shelter. The two detectives rang the doorbell and no one answered. I was told to open the door with my key. One of the detectives told me to start walking up the stairs. He pulled out his gun and walked behind me. If Ken fired, he didn't want to be the target. Sure! Great protection! I couldn't believe what was happening. When I was halfway up the stairs, Ken opened the door at the top of the stairs and stood before us in his underwear holding his shotgun sideways in his hands. What a bloody nightmare! I froze. The detective yelled at Ken that he had three seconds to throw his gun to the floor. Ken just stared at the detective. The detective repeated himself and then Ken threw the gun down saying he was only cleaning it and called him a fool.

I entered the house with the two detectives and one police officer. They told Ken he had five minutes to pack his things and leave. They told him he was supposed to leave a couple days prior and that the judge had given him three days. Ken was stalling, so the police officer told him if he didn't hurry up he was going to escort him out in his underwear. Ken packed a few things and had the nerve to ask the police officer for a lift to his mother's. The officer declined. As Ken was walking down the stairs, I could see from the window that there were neighbours gathered outside my house. Once Ken emerged from the house, all of the neighbors started clapping loudly. I was so embarrassed. Ten minutes later, I was escorted back to the shelter to pick up Wendy and Keith.

It felt great to be back home. I was still very nervous because I knew the fight for my freedom had just begun. There would be many court dates coming up. Wayne kept being transferred from one detention centre to another. He started stealing cars and getting fraudulent credit cards. He also was breaking into people houses and stealing. He had started a life of crime.

Noella and Peter, my neighbours and friends across the street, were the ones driving me to and from court. They would also pay for my lunches time and time again when we had long court days. I truly believe they were sent by

God to help me start a new life. A life I wasn't living. I was merely existing. I prayed to God on a daily basis to help me, and I see today that it was through them that he answered my prayers.

In between court dates, Ken started sending his threatening telegrams again. All were sent in a way where there wasn't any proof it was him. He made sure the threats could never stand up in court. During all of this nonsense, the court ordered me to bring Keith for supervised visits to see his father. The visits were to be in a social worker's office, once every two weeks for one hour. The visits lasted a couple of weeks and then Ken just stopped showing up.

I landed a babysitting job and the lady agreed I could bring Keith with me. With the extra money now coming in, we started to eat and dress a lot better. Wayne started to come around the house again. He was breaking my heart as he was so mixed up and hurting inside. He would call me a lot of names and I wouldn't stand for it, so I had to tell him to go. All I wanted to do was give him a big hug and a kiss and tell him I loved him.

On February 13th, 1986, Ken applied for the custody of Wayne. I will never forget that day in court. Mr. Butenski, who was our social worker at the time, came into the courtroom white as a ghost. He told the judge that Ken had pulled a gun on him, threatening him to testify that Wayne should be placed with his father. All of a sudden, all the doors in the courtroom were locked. Ken was arrested and taken off to jail. We spent the whole day in court for nothing as the whole entire building was searched, and the police never found Ken's gun.

Ken was released from jail the very next morning. He started sending me bills for the food and clothes he and his mother were buying for Wayne when he was there. Wayne was in between detention centres but would always take off and then go stay at his grandmother's with his dad. I just ignored the bills. There was one bill I couldn't believe I received. Since I stopped taking Keith to see his father at the social worker's office because he never showed, they decided to fine me $200. I did not pay this fine. As far as I was concerned, the judge was as crazy as Ken was. I went to the court and explained my financial situation. The amount was dropped.

Ken was now wanted for over twenty cases of fraud involving several different banks. The amount he owed was over three thousand dollars. He actually got Shawn involved with the fraud and my son had to go to court for this. They both pleaded guilty. The judge gave Ken two years' probation and one full year to pay back the money. Shawn was given one year of probation.

I was starting to look so old. I was depressed and neglecting myself. It was so hard to get motivated again and be happy. So many times I wanted to die. Having no love in my life, being lonely and poor didn't help my situation. Mark and Shawn were never there to support me. I understand now that they probably didn't want any part in all of the crazy drama.

It was now June 28th, 1989. It had been exactly one year that I had been out of the woman's shelter. I received a phone call from Ken asking me to marry him. I couldn't believe he was on the phone. I had changed my phone number four times and had it unlisted. How did he get the number? He said he was sick and needed me. He said he missed me and if I told him yes, he would be at my place within five minutes. I was numb all over. I asked him how he had retrieved my number and he said he had his ways. He told me it didn't matter how many times I would change it because he would get it again. He told me to stop wasting my money. I knew this man was crazy but that topped the cake. Very calmly, I told Ken no, I would not marry him, and that if he felt he really was sick then he didn't need me, he needed to see a doctor. I asked him very politely to stop calling the house.

The minute I hung up the phone he started calling nonstop. Wendy got very upset at this and started crying.

I tried to console her as much as I possibly could. Eventually, he stopped calling, but I did wonder for how long.

A month passed and Noella and Peter invited us up to their country place. I took Wendy and Keith along. Wayne was still with his father and Shawn and Mark were doing their own thing. I agreed to go and get a break from everything that was going on. I needed peace as a reason to go on. It was beautiful there. I felt like a teenager again. We made bonfires and the kids took walks with Peter in the woods. I stayed with Noella and talked. She gave me the inner strength to go back and face Ken again. She reassured me everything was going to work out. She said she would always stand by me and help me in any way she could. She was a real friend. Someone who cared and fought hard for what she believed in She was compassionate yet fierce at the same time. She wouldn't stand for anyone's bullshit and would tell you right away. That is the reason why Ken disliked her. He knew he couldn't get away with anything with her. I actually think he was a bit leery of her!

October 1986 came around and I had twenty-four cents left in my bank account. I needed five dollars and ten cents to keep the account open. I telephone some relatives, including my mother, for some help and they all turned me down. I was now forty-six years old and had five children to raise on a small welfare cheque. How was I going to do it? I didn't

have a job but sure needed one fast. Wendy would complain
because I didn't have any money to give her. Wayne had been
sentenced to one year at the Cité des Prairies detention centre
because he had threatened his peers, and he was expelled
from summer camp because of the verbal abuse and threats
he'd made to staff members. Wayne had also blackmailed
another boy who was placed in a different centre. He had
a lot of behavioral problems and was lashing out at anyone
and everyone.

Wayne stayed at Cité des Prairies until February of 1987.
I visited him quite often. He had a little bed in his cell. It
broke my heart to hear that he had to sleep in a locked cell,
but Wayne was out of control and for now it had to be that
way. He did go to school there; they had a nice library and
TV room and also a gym. Taking one look at him you could
tell his heart was broken. He used to always ask me to bring
his girlfriend up there. He, too, was soul-searching and
wanted love. Ken and I had let him down. I felt so useless.
I could hardly get my life together, let alone help him.

Ville-Marie social services were the ones that let me down.
A year had passed and Wayne was finally released from Cité
des Prairies. Ken had received temporary custody of him
until our court case. I couldn't believe it. It didn't make any
sense at all. I was sure Ken had once again threatened all
the social workers, because who in their right mind would

release my son into the arms of his sick and twisted father? When I found out the news I cried for days. Wayne was on a strict curfew. He was forced to attend school and be in the house before dark. He wasn't allowed to hang around with the friends he had before. They wanted him to have a fresh start. We all wanted that for Wayne. He deserved it. All of my children did.

March 14th, 1988: my day in court to get my divorce was finally here. Proceedings went as planned and I received my divorce and was granted full custody of the five children. Ken had no visitation rights whatsoever. I knew that would not last long when it came to seeing Wayne, but at least I had the papers from the court if anything was to happen. Wayne was old enough that I couldn't force him not to see his father, but I did hope he would stay away. I wanted to see all my children happy, and being around their father wasn't going to help make that happen.

Mark was always at his girlfriend's house down the street. Shawn was always with his friends, Kyle and Jarred. Wayne was either with his father or all of the friends he had. Wendy was also getting very attached to all her girlfriends. I was the least important person in all their lives. I knew there was nothing I could do about that, but I didn't like the feeling at all.

By June of 1988 I had landed a few more cleaning jobs. I was able to put Keith in the after-school program. It didn't cost a lot, and because of this I was able to bring home some extra money. It felt good to be able to provide a little more for the children. I never asked for much. I just wanted to be able to provide for my family and get them a treat every once in a while.

THE SHOOTING

ONE NIGHT I WAS AWAKENED BY NOISES THAT sounded like firecrackers. I looked out my window and didn't see anything. I then went to the kitchen and made a cup of coffee. All was still afterward, so I eventually went back to sleep. The next day after work, I picked Keith up after school as usual. When I arrived home, no one was there. Wendy wasn't home from school yet. The telephone rang and it was Mark. He was calling from his girlfriend's house. Mark had moved into Melody's house with her parents a couple months back. He told me to sit down. He said he had bad news about Wayne.

I immediately start to panic. Mark told me that Wayne has been shot by a police officer and he was in the Montreal Children's Hospital in intensive care. I immediately dropped the phone. Tears filled my eyes. My son was shot? I couldn't believe it. I picked the receiver back up and Mark told me not to worry. He said the doctor said that he was young and strong and he was going to pull through. He said he was going to come and pick me up and we would go and see him together.

I made Wendy babysit Keith that day. While I was in the car, Mark started to tell me what had happened. Wayne and another boy were in Crawford Park stealing a car. The keys were accidently left in the car so that made for an easy steal. The firecracker noise I heard the night before were the shots fired from the police officer shooting my boy! Wayne's friend was the one in the stolen car and Wayne was driving his friend's car. When the police arrived at the scene, they yelled at Wayne to stop the car and Wayne didn't, and this is the reason he was shot. Once the officer fired, Wayne panicked and took off. He didn't see that there was another police officer in front of him, and he hit him, causing the officer to go flying over the hood of the car. Little did I know that my son was facing an attempted murder charge.

Mark parked the car and we went into the hospital. I ran so fast to the elevator. Wayne was on the 15th floor. I was praying to God he was awake and alive. We found Wayne's room and, to my surprise, I couldn't enter right away. He was in intensive care. A police officer was guarding the door. He made us sign our name going in and also sign out when we left. What was this all about? I didn't question it at the time because all I wanted to do was get in the room and see my boy. Only family was permitted to see Wayne. After we signed in, we went over to Wayne's bedside. My son was shackled to the bed with chains. There was another officer right by his bedside. I was told this was standard procedure because Wayne was being charged with the attempted murder of a police officer. As my son lay there unconscious, I could not help but cry. My poor little boy, only seventeen years old, already in trouble with the law and lying in a hospital bed clinging to his life.

"Wayne, can you hear me?" I said. I begged the Lord not to take my son. I begged for him to wake up. I didn't understand how a cop could shoot my teenage son in the stomach and through his spleen. He was supposed to shoot the tires to stop the car, not my boy. A little while later, Wayne opened his eyes. He was very groggy for a while but he did manage a couple of words. He told me he thought he killed a police officer. I knew he was still drugged up on morphine. I told him not to worry and to rest. I kissed him on his forehead. It was so heartbreaking seeing my son lying in a hospital bed with multiple gunshot wounds. He was so swollen and had an oxygen mask to help him breathe. He stayed in intensive care for about two weeks. The police officers gradually took off the shackles and just kept a guard in the room with a police officer standing guard outside at all times.

After about two and a half weeks, Wayne was considered out of danger and the hospital staff took him out of intensive care and transferred him to his own room. I went to visit him as often as I could. Ken was at the hospital every single day. On the days I was not able to make it, he would make sarcastic remarks that I didn't come every day and insinuated that I was a bad mother. I ignored all his stupid remarks because my only concern was that my son recovered.

One day Wayne took a turn for the worst. His stomach started filling up with blood. There was a leakage in the main artery to his heart. They had to act fast. Wayne needed surgery right away. They rushed him in to the OR and we all waited. The operation seemed to take forever. I was so nervous I must have smoked over a pack of cigarettes that day. We were told that everything went well but he needed a lot of rest and wasn't able to see anyone until the next day. Pacing back and forth while my son was in the operating room, I started thinking. I started thinking of all the things I could have done differently in my life. If I had, could I have avoided all of this?

Being at the hospital so much, I used to take breaks and get snacks at the cafeteria. One day while I was sitting in there, I overheard some nurses and doctors talking about Wayne. They were gossiping about how he had killed a police officer. They said there was going to be a bail hearing upstairs at the hospital because my son was actually under arrest, but they had to wait until he was well enough to attend the hearing. I didn't say a word and I assumed they didn't realize I was his mother. How did I not know this? Why didn't anyone ever tell me anything? I went back upstairs and questioned the police officer outside of Wayne's room and he confirmed this was true. He told me that before Wayne could leave the hospital, there was going to be a bail hearing. If he was convicted, he would go straight from the hospital to jail. The nurse came into the room later that day and told me that Wayne needed a second operation. He was still recovering from the first one. She told us that they had to repair the main aorta to Wayne's heart. I was devastated. How much more pain could my son bear? Looking at him was getting more difficult each day. With each operation, Wayne would be left with more holes from where the tubes had been. These open wounds took long to heal. He must have had ten to fifteen holes all around his mid-section. He asked how bad it looked, and I always reassured him everything was fine and he was healing well. My son was in the hospital for a total of eight months. He had to learn to walk all over again. Wayne had a walker that he used to wheel down to a room where he would get physiotherapy to help him be able to walk. He did exercises to help strengthen his legs and different ones for his arms. Every time he went, the police officer would follow. It was horrible.

Wayne finally had a bail hearing at the hospital. The judge actually came along with Wayne's lawyer. Before the hearing started, Wayne asked me if he could come home and heal. He said he needed three months to do so. I told him of course he could come home. It was a pretty emotional conversation. He squeezed my hand from his bed and thanked me.

The bail hearing lasted about two hours. Wayne was refused bail. He was told he would have another hearing in a month. Wayne was so upset. He told me that Ken was driving the staff at the hospital crazy. Ken was demanding special attention for Wayne and also meals for himself. The staff was so fed up with Ken that he was asked to leave and escorted out of the hospital by a security guard.

THE RECOVERY

WAYNE WAS HEALING SLOWLY, HIS SPLEEN HAD BEEN removed and he was doing his physio daily, trying to regain strength. It would take some time for his open wounds to heal, but nothing was infected so this was a good sign. The day came for his second bail hearing. I went to the hospital early that morning. I walked into the cafeteria as I always did before going to Wayne's room. Once again, I overheard all the nurses and doctors gossiping about my son. They were making him out to be a cold-hearted cop killer. I wanted so badly to scream at them and tell them the real story, but I kept my cool. I was just praying he would make bail and be able to come home.

As I entered Wayne's hospital room, a chill came over my body. I was so nervous for my son. There stood Ken, Wayne's lawyer, a police officer and two guards. Wayne was in his bed, lying there and looking so thin and helpless. The lawyer was on the phone the whole time with the judge, I believe, because the judge was not present this time. After about twenty minutes, the lawyer got off the phone and looked at Wayne and told him his bail was granted. Wayne was very happy. I saw the relief on his face. This was only temporary, though, because Wayne was facing a lot of charges. He was being charged with possession of a stolen vehicle, reckless driving, violation of curfew and attempted murder of a police officer.

Wayne came home the following day. It felt wonderful having all the children together. I just wanted to help Wayne heal. I wanted to try and talk to him. Hopefully put some sense into his head and let him know that a life of crime wasn't a life. To show him he could have a better life here at home with us.

Every day, I had to clean and sterilize all the holes in Wayne's chest and stomach that were left from the bullet wounds, as well as the holes from his tubes. I had sterile gloves, tweezers, scissors and gauze. My daily routine was to get up, take care of Wayne, send Keith off to school and then go to my cleaning jobs. I would be back in time to tend to Wayne in the early afternoon. The cleaning jobs never took more than four hours, so this was quite convenient for me.

As Wayne healed, he started to have a complex about his holes. He kept taking off his shirt and staring at them in the mirror. I tried to reassure him, saying that in time they would heal and he would get chest hair that would cover them up, but my talks didn't seem to help. He stayed in the house most of the time. He started to ask if his friends could come over. I didn't like the crowd Wayne hung with but I said yes to him anyway. I wish he would have changed his friends and made new friends who were quiet and had goals in life.

The French newspaper *La Presse* had written a big article on Wayne and the police shooting. They had published pictures of Wayne's chest and detailed how the police had shot him. Wayne was in the process of suing the police officer, so this is why it made headlines. All of my neighbours and friends were coming to the house to console me. It was a very emotional time.

The day came for Wayne to go to court and face the charges against him. The court was packed. There was a lot of security in and outside the courtroom. When it was time for the police officer who shot Wayne to enter courtroom, Ken ran up to him behind his back and pointed his finger at his back yelling, "Make my day!" This was a saying Ken heard in a movie once. The police officer didn't even flinch and kept walking towards the stand. There were rumours that the same police officer had shot other kids, as well. We didn't have names or proof. It was all just hearsay, but why the rumours? I believed Wayne's story that it was truly an unjust shooting. The police officer testified what happened to him. He did it without any emotion at all. He seemed heartless and monotone. Everyone had their turn to testify, including Wayne. Hearing his testimony broke my heart. I held back my tears as I wanted to hear the full story once and for all. It was hard as a mother to hear awful things about your son. After all the testimony was over, we left to go home. The judge wasn't making a decision right away. He had to think about the case and was going to mail out another date for us to come back so he could render his decision.

Less than twelve hours after testifying before the Quebec police commissioner about being shot and abused by police, Wayne was arrested for stealing another car. Wayne could kiss the lawsuit against the police goodbye as the minute he stole another car, it went down the drain. How could he do this? What was he thinking? I understood he had been moulded by the teachings of his father from a very young age and hung around with friends who also did this type of crime, but what was it going to take for Wayne to get the help he needed? I was so afraid for my son—afraid for his life at this point. He ended up doing time in a juvenile detention centre on the car theft charges only. He called me on and off, but I knew it would take some time for Wayne to realize that a life of crime wasn't worth it.

Wendy had a lot of problems in school. She was rude to the teachers and always fighting with schoolmates. It was so bad that she was expelled when she was in grade nine. The principal didn't want her returning ever again. I went to a meeting with her that I was called to attend. She insisted she had changed and wanted to try again, but I felt she needed the change and I agreed with the principal that she should not return. She was very angry at me. She felt that I let her down by not fighting for her to stay in that school. Eventually, she enrolled in the adult education program at another school to get her high school diploma.

THE LIGHT AT THE END
OF THE TUNNEL

Mark started making wedding plans with another girlfriend he had met. His first girlfriend, Melody, didn't last because he had issues with her parents. He was now going to marry a lovely girl named Christine. Shawn, my second oldest, was also living on his own and working. Wayne was still in and out of trouble. Wendy was enrolled at her new school, and Keith, my youngest, was spared from most of the dreadful drama and abuse of Ken. I had a lot more cleaning jobs and even started taking college courses in Early Childhood Development, with the hope of opening a daycare one day.

Ken's threats and annoying behaviour became less and less. I found out through the boys that he had a girlfriend. God help her, I thought in my mind. It was a great thing because the more he concentrated on his new girlfriend, the less he would bother us. I started to date again. It felt great. I felt alive. Wendy, however, didn't like the fact she had to babysit Keith. She was becoming more and more intolerable to live with. It reached a point where I had to put her out. She was just seventeen at the time and I contacted the Ville-Marie Social Service Centre to place her in a home. She immediately got a job and her own place with a friend, so they advised me there was nothing they could do.

I was left with just Keith now and I eventually moved into another place that was suitable for the two of us. Ken continued living with his mother until she died, and then he moved in with his sick aunt. He could never make it on his own alone. He gave up on life, didn't have a friend in the world and lost all of the respect from his children except for Wayne. Wayne always felt sorry for his father and probably will until the day he dies.

I, however, flourished. I worked hard to live a peaceful life. I never thought I would end up being happy. I found love a couple of years later and married a man named Bob. He was a gentle and loving man. I had ten wonderful years with him before he passed away of heart failure.

In a lifetime, we may experience many different obstacles. Obstacles that might make us feel like giving up or that might make us feel helpless. I want every woman who reads this book to remember, YOU ARE NOT ALONE. There is help out there. Every family is going through something.

They might not talk about it, but they are. Please remember that you are loved and you WILL be able to get through it. Talking is the key; the more we talk, the faster we will be able to figure out what the next step is.

I hope you enjoyed my story, and I hope it will help women all around the world know that they CAN make it through even during the darkest of times. And in the end, there is a light at the end of the tunnel.

God Bless,

Ann Augustine